GD'S
COVENANT
With YOU
FOR YOUR FAMILY

JOHN
ECKHARDT

CHARISMA
HOUSE

Most CHARISMA HOUSE BOOK GROUP products are available at special quantity discounts for bulk purchase for sales promotions, premiums, fund-raising, and educational needs. For details, write Charisma House Book Group, 600 Rinehart Road, Lake Mary, Florida 32746, or telephone (407) 333-0600.

GOD'S COVENANT WITH YOU FOR YOUR FAMILY
   by John Eckhardt
Published by Charisma House
Charisma Media/Charisma House Book Group
600 Rinehart Road
Lake Mary, Florida 32746
www.charismahouse.com

Unless otherwise noted, all Scripture quotations are from the New King James Version of the Bible.

Scripture quotations marked GNT are from the Good News Translation. Copyright © 1992 by American Bible Society. Used by permission.

Scripture quotations marked KJV are from the King James Version of the Bible.

Scripture quotations marked NIV are from the Holy Bible, New International Version. Copyright © 1973, 1978, 1984, International Bible Society. Used by permission.

Cover design by Justin Evans
Design Director: Bill Johnson

Visit the author's website at www.johneckhardtministries.com.

Library of Congress Cataloging-in-Publication Data:
An application to register this book for cataloging has been
submitted to the Library of Congress.
International Standard Book Number: 978-1-62136-012-4
E-book ISBN: 978-1-62136-013-1

While the author has made every effort to provide accurate
telephone numbers and Internet addresses at the time of
publication, neither the publisher nor the author assumes any
responsibility for errors or for changes that occur after publication.

First edition

13 14 15 16 17 — 9 8 7 6 5 4 3 2 1
Printed in the United States of America

CONTENTS

1

GOD BLESSES FAMILIES THROUGH HIS COVENANT

[Covenant is] probably the least understood, yet most important concept in the entire Bible... and is at once the heart and the foundation of mankind's relationship with God.

—J. E. LEONARD[1]

THE BIBLE IS a covenantal book that reveals a covenantal God. God's loyalty and faithfulness to covenant is one of the major themes of Scripture. From the Old Testament to the New Testament we see God working His covenant on behalf of His people. God cannot break covenant. God is faithful and loyal to His people.

We can trust and rely on God's covenant because He is committed to His promises. When a covenant is made, the person enacting the covenant would swear by someone higher than himself. This was so that if the covenant was ever broken, that person would be judged and held accountable to the person higher than him. When God first established His covenant with man, He could swear by no one higher, so He swore by Himself.

> For when God made promise to Abraham, because He could swear by no greater, He swore by Himself.
> —HEBREWS 6:13

God is the highest. There is no one greater than Him. This means we can absolutely trust, rely upon, and depend upon our covenant with God. God cannot lie. He will remain faithful to His Word.

A biblical covenant is an agreement—generally between God and man. The stipulations of such an agreement command absolute loyalty as indicated in the first commandment: "You shall not have other gods before Me" (Exod. 20:3; Deut. 5:7).

Covenant (berit/berith/beriyth) means "treaty, compact, agreement between two parties (first used in God's covenant with Noah—Genesis 6:18; 9:9–17). As discussed more below *beriyth* describes a compact made by passing between pieces of flesh. Covenant is a solemn, binding arrangement between two parties and entails a variety of responsibilities, benefits and penalties depending on the specific covenant, which is being studied."[2]

God enters into covenant with men. This is a very humbling and sobering truth. The fact that the great God would enter into relationship with men through covenant is amazing. God's purposes are always done through covenant. God's covenant with Abraham was for the purpose of bringing salvation and blessing to the nations. God's covenant with Israel was also for this purpose: to bring the Messiah into the world. I want to explain this more and will in chapter 3 when we talk about household salvation. Right now let's uncover the truths of the new covenant that we are now walking in as believers.

THE NEW COVENANT IS A COVENANT OF PEACE AND PROSPERITY

If the household is worthy, let your peace come upon it. But if it is not worthy, let your peace return to you.
—MATTHEW 10:13

The new covenant is a covenant of peace (*shalom*). Christ is our peace. When salvation comes to a family, God's peace (shalom) will also come.

We often associate the word *shalom* with *peace*, but the peace that Christ went to war for on the cross is a complete, whole kind of peace. According to *Strong's Complete Concordance to the Bible*, *shalom* is "completeness, soundness, welfare, and peace." It represents completeness in number and safety and soundness in your physical body. *Shalom* also covers relationships with God and with people. *Shalom* covers all that concerns you and your family.

God's thoughts concerning you and your family's peace and prosperity are much higher than you could imagine. It is His desire to bless and prosper you, to give you His grace, favor, and protection. *Favor* means "grace"; "that which affords joy, pleasure, delight, sweetness, charm, loveliness"; and "good will, benefit, bounty, reward." If you look up the Hebrew and Greek definitions of *prosperity*, many of these words carry over into favor as well.

Favor is goodwill. This is God's kindness and benevolence given to those who love Him. Favor will release great blessings, including prosperity, health, opportunity, and advancement. The Bible records numerous examples of God's favor upon His people causing them to experience many breakthroughs. Favor is God's loving-kindness. I want you will get the full revelation of all that God's covenant of peace can mean for you and your family.

God's peace (shalom)—favor, grace, loving-kindness, blessing, goodness, joy, prosperity, health, opportunity, and advancement—can come upon your house. God desires to bring the fullness of His shalom to your house. Many houses are filled with strife and confusion. Alcoholism, drug addiction, strife, division, depression, sadness, anger, divorce, separation, and bitterness dwell in many homes, but this is not God's plan. This is opposite to the characteristics of the kingdom of God, which are righteousness, *peace*, and joy in the Holy Spirit (Rom. 14:17).

One of the descriptions of our covenant is "a covenant of *shalom*." *Shalom* describes the benefits and blessing of this covenant. In Isaiah 54 God promised His people a covenant of peace (shalom): "For the mountains shall depart, and the hills be removed; but my kindness shall not depart from thee, neither shall the covenant of my peace be removed, saith the Lord that hath mercy on thee" (v. 10, KJV). But Israel never walked in that covenant of peace consistently because they continued to violate it. The greatest period of shalom was under King Solomon, whose name actually means peace. He was the most prosperous king of Israel. For a forty-year period Israel lived under that promise of shalom. But then Solomon married other wives and took part in idolatry, and there was a breech or a split from the covenant God had established.

Peace, or shalom, comes from God. Only He can give it, and He can take it away. We also have the choice to be blessed by walking in covenant with Him or to deactivate it by not walking in covenant with Him.

> I form the light and create darkness, I make peace and create calamity; I, the LORD, do all these things.
> —ISAIAH 45:7

When you leave God and break His covenant, God will withdraw His shalom, and He will allow disaster. The enemy will come into your land and destroy you. The sword will come in the land, and prosperity will be destroyed. We see that this is true based on the Israelites' experience all through the Book of Judges. But God will send warning and correction. He began to send prophets or "covenant messengers" to a covenant people to warn them of their covenant violation to give them a chance to repent before God's covenant wrath would come upon them. The prophets repeatedly said that there is no peace to the wicked (Isa. 48:22; 57:21).

If a prophet tells you that you will have a life of peace and you are violating God's Word—His covenant—the prophet is lying, because you will not experience shalom or peace or prosperity if you are not living in covenant with God. When someone is wicked and unrighteous, he or she is not at peace. Do not be fooled.

ONLY ONE WAY TO TRUE PEACE

God promised Israel that if they would keep His commandments, He would give them that shalom. But they did not listen. However, God had a plan that would restore Israel, if they chose. And His plan would extend to all mankind.

In Jeremiah 31:31–34 God told the people that they would not be able to experience His peace under the old covenant because they continued to break it. He was alluding to the fact that they would only be able to experience God's true peace by way of the Messiah. The Messiah would come to make a new covenant. He came preaching the good news of the kingdom.

The only way you can experience the true shalom of God is through His Son—the "Prince of Peace" (Isa. 9:6). Jesus came preaching the "gospel of peace" (Rom. 10:15; Eph. 6:15)—or the gospel of shalom, the gospel of the kingdom. So we have to repent and receive the gospel of peace.

You are under a new covenant when you have accepted Christ's sacrifice for you and submit your life under His authority. But when you reject Christ and His sacrifice, you reject His new covenant and the very shalom you are looking for—as the children of Israel rejected Him when He came. In Luke 19:41–42 Jesus cried over Jerusalem because He knew that if they rejected Him, they would not experience shalom but instead experience the sword. He knew that the enemy would build a trench around them and would besiege them on every side and not one stone would be left one upon another. War, famine, poverty, pestilence, and death were coming.

When you reject Jesus, you reject your only hope for peace and prosperity.

GOD ESTABLISHED A COVENANT SO THAT HE COULD BLESS YOU

You must understand how much God wants to bless His people with peace. He is the God of peace. He is Jehovah Shalom. He is the Lord our prosperity. But Israel couldn't see what was right in front of their eyes and missed it. So now this blessing belongs to the new covenant church. We inherit the promise of shalom—prosperity, favor, peace, health, and safety—because we are the ones who, through the blood of Jesus, enter into a new covenant with God. What Israel could not receive in the natural we receive in the spirit. It now belongs to you and your family!

Covenant means "faithfulness." Husband and wife have to be faithful to each other. Divorce comes into the picture because a covenant has been broken. Keep a covenant relationship with God. There is a huge advantage to doing this: blessing comes with covenant. God does not just bless people for any reason. Being in covenant with God is a contract or a promise of His peace, safety, favor, protection, health, and prosperity. And God does not break His promises or go back on His word (Num. 23:19; Isa. 55:11).

Covenant with God is a mutual blessing. God gets a people, and we get God (Lev. 26:12). However, when God doesn't get a people, there is no need for the covenant. We cannot be God's own if we do not walk according to His covenant. He cannot claim us and put His name on us. We can pray for peace all year long, but without Jesus, who is the Prince of Peace, shalom will never come.

> To all who are in Rome, beloved of God, called to be saints: Grace to you and peace [prosperity, shalom] from God our Father and the Lord Jesus Christ.
>
> —ROMANS 1:7

Notice whom the peace goes to. This peace is not to a physical people, but to those "called to be saints." The saints possess the kingdom of God. Are you a saint? This goes beyond being saved. The saints are the holy ones. It doesn't mean that you are perfect or that you don't make mistakes. It means that your lifestyle is holy. You don't *live* a sinful lifestyle. In the New Testament the saints walked in a level of holiness. They were not liars, drunkards, or whoremongers. They didn't mistreat people. If you are not a saint, you are not saved. The verse says, "Grace [*charis*, favor] and peace to those who are called to be saints." If you are a saint, prosperity belongs to you, not because of anything you did or didn't do, but because of what Jesus did for us all on Calvary. That is the blood covenant.

Shalom is the Hebrew word usually translated "peace," which means prosperity, harmony (within and without), completeness, wholeness, health, welfare, safety, soundness, tranquility, fullness, rest, the absence of agitation or discord, a state of calm without anxiety or stress.

PEACE IS THE HALLMARK OF THE KINGDOM

God has given us His covenant of shalom and will not go back on it.

"For the mountains shall depart, and the hills be removed, but My kindness shall not depart from you, nor shall My covenant of peace be removed," says the Lord, who has mercy on you.

　　　　　　　　　　　　　　　　　　　—Isaiah 54:10

The new covenant is a covenant of shalom (peace). Shalom is the hallmark of the kingdom. A hallmark is a conspicuous characteristic or feature. This should be a characteristic of those living in the kingdom. Consider these verses that spoke of the arrival of the kingdom.

He shall judge between the nations, and rebuke many people; they shall beat their swords into plowshares, and their spears into pruning hooks; nation shall not lift up sword against nation, neither shall they learn war any more.

　　　　　　　　　　　　　　　　　　　—Isaiah 2:4

Peace (shalom) is the result of the arrival of the kingdom. Swords turn into plowshares, and spears into pruning hooks. Instead of learning war, men walk in peace. It is not the will of God for strife, division, bitterness, anger, and hatred to destroy your family. The peace of God can rule in your family.

For unto us a Child is born, unto us a Son is given; and the government shall be upon His shoulder. And His name will be called Wonderful, Counsellor, Mighty God, Everlasting Father, Prince of Peace [shalom]. Of the increase of His government and peace [shalom] there will be no end, upon the throne of David and over His kingdom, to order it and establish it with judgment and

justice from that time forward, even forever. The zeal of
the LORD of hosts will perform this.

—ISAIAH 9:6–7

The government of God increases from generation to generation. This can include you, your family, and your descendants. The
gospel is the good news of peace (shalom). The gospel brings the
peace of God into a family.

How beautiful upon the mountains are the feet of him
who brings good news, who proclaims peace [shalom],
who brings good tidings of good things, who proclaims
salvation, who says to Zion, "Your God reigns!"

—ISAIAH 52:7

When the gospel (good news) of Jesus is accepted by a believer,
the door is opened for the gospel to enter the person's family. I
believe this is a powerful way of kingdom increase and expansion.
God has designed the family unit to be a place where the gospel
can spread and the kingdom can increase.

WHAT COVENANT WITH GOD
BRINGS TO KINGDOM FAMILIES

Every believer needs a revelation of the covenantal faithfulness and
mercy of God. Every believer needs a revelation of the benefits of
covenant. A revelation of covenant will take your relationship with
God to whole new levels. You will begin to see the faithfulness,
loyalty, and commitment of God to His people. You will trust the
Lord with a whole new sense of understanding. When you have
a revelation of covenant, the whole context of the Bible changes
for you. Things that seemed piecemeal or unrelated will have new

continuity and significance. You will see everything through the context of covenant—from the Old Testament (shadows and symbols) to the New Testament (fullness and reality).

Believers with a clear revelation of covenant have the confidence to understand what is rightfully theirs. Their prayers, supplications, and requests will be made in faith and without doubt because they understand their agreement with the Lord. They will understand that their healing and deliverance are not based on what they do or don't do; they are based on covenant, on the covenantal mercy of God. They understand that God is connected with them and has covenanted with them through Jesus Christ.

When you stand in prayer for healing, blessing, and favor for your family, you will have a new level of authority and faith because you understand covenant. You will see your commitment to God and His commitment to you. You will understand that it is His covenantal love that loads you with the benefits of His covenant.

> Blessed be the Lord, who daily loads us with benefits, the God of our salvation. Selah.
>
> —Psalm 68:19

> Bless the Lord, O my soul, and forget not all his benefits.
> —Psalm 103:2

> What shall I render to the Lord for all his benefits toward me?
>
> —Psalm 116:12

To bless means "to invoke divine favor on, to bestow happiness, prosperity or good things of all kinds; to make a pronouncement holy; to consecrate, to glorify for the benefits received, to extol for excellencies."[3] Likewise a blessing is "a prayer or solemn wish imploring happiness upon another; a benediction or blessing; the act of pronouncing a benediction or blessing; that which promotes prosperity and welfare."[4] Then in the Hebrew language, "to bless" is the word *barak*, which means "to kneel by implication to bless God as an act of adoration, to praise, salute, thanks…a posture of reverence."[5] And again the word *blessing* in Hebrew is *berakah*, which is a "benediction (an act of invoking a blessing)."[6]

The Lord, through His covenant, wants to shower His blessing and benefits on your family. Here are some of the ways He will do it.

- The covenant of peace means your children are taught of the Lord. Claim this for your children and your descendants (Isa. 54:13).

- Your family members who are far off will experience the peace of God. God's peace will come to the nations. The families of the earth will experience the peace of God (Isa. 57:19).

- God's peace will flow into your family like a river. God's presence (sanctuary) will manifest in your family. God's presence brings peace. God multiplies us. Multiplication is a symbol of God's blessing (Ezek. 37:26).

- Christ is our peace (shalom). The new covenant is based on the finished work of Christ. When salvation (Christ) comes into a family, the blessing of peace (shalom) comes (Eph. 2:14).

- The Lord will prosper your family. He delights in our prosperity. In other words, God *wants* your family (servants) to prosper (Ps. 35:27; 122:7; 147:14).

As I mentioned briefly above, the word *shalom* is also translated "prosperity." God prospers families. Our covenant gives us the right to enjoy the peace and prosperity of the kingdom. Settle for nothing less than shalom. This is your covenant right. Claim it and walk in it today. There is no end to the increase of peace (shalom) from generation to generation. Family salvations will bring an increase to the kingdom and the peace of God.

- God's covenant of peace brings healing and restoration of families (Isa. 57:19).
- God's covenant will bring not only peace but also an abundance of peace to your family (Ps. 37:11).
- God's covenant will cause your family to flourish (Ps. 72:7).
- God's covenant will bring joy, peace, and singing to your family (Isa. 55:12).
- God's covenant will release His mercy to your family (Deut. 7:9; Neh. 1:5; 9:32; Ps. 25:10; 89:24, 28; 106:45).
- God's covenant will release His faithfulness, loyalty, and steadfastness to your family (Deut. 7:9; Ps. 118:1, 5–6; 1 Cor. 1:9).

God is the faithful God. Faithfulness is a mark of covenant. God is always faithful to His people and His promises.

God was always faithful to the families of Israel in spite of their unfaithfulness. God kept His covenant with Abraham and brought forth His seed (Jesus) to bless the nations. God was faithful to Israel and sent Jesus to them first to bless them. God was faithful to the house of David and caused David's son to sit on his throne. The Lord will endure forever with His covenant families.

The word *steadfast* means, "firmly fixed in place, immovable, not subject to change." The word *endure* means: "to continue in the same state, last, to remain firm under suffering or misfortune without yielding." The word *forever* means, "for a limitless time, at all times, continually." Hence, the meaning of each of these key words speaks to us of the powerful, firm, trustworthy, tenacious, never-ending love of God.

THE COVENANTAL NAMES OF GOD

Israel enjoyed the benefits of God throughout their history because of covenant. God revealed Himself through His covenantal names.

There are eight covenant names by which God revealed Himself and His purpose to Israel. These names comprehend the benefits God made available to Israel through His covenant. Whoever knew those names and called upon God based on the names they represented had God's promise that He would behave toward them in the fashion demanded by each of His titles. Your family can begin to incorporate these names when you call upon the Lord in prayer.

Here are the names listed in the order of their historical relation to Israel:

1. Yahweh-Jireh, the Lord our Provider (Gen. 22:8, 14)

2. Yahweh-Rapha, the Lord our Healer (Exod. 15:26)

3. Yahweh-Nissi, the Lord our Banner (Exod. 17:15)

4. Yahweh-Qadesh, the Lord our Sanctifier (Lev. 20:8; Ezek. 20:12)

5. Yahweh-Shalom, the Lord our Peace (Judg. 6:24)

6. Yahweh-Raah, the Lord our Shepherd (Ps. 23:1)

7. Yahweh-Tsidkenu, the Lord our Righteousness (Jer. 23:6)

8. Yahweh-Shammah, the Lord Ever Present (Ezek. 48:35)

All of these names are fulfilled in Jesus. Jesus is our healer, provider, banner, sanctifier, peace, shepherd, righteousness, and ever-present One. In other words, all the fullness of God is manifested through the name of Jesus.

Jesus Is Our Covenant

Salvation through Jesus can drive out demons from families. As individuals in the family accept Christ, deliverance comes and family strongholds are broken. Generational curses are broken, and generational spirits are cast out.

Christ is our peace (shalom).

> For He Himself is our peace, who has made both one, and has broken down the middle wall of separation.
> —Ephesians 2:14

Christ is Jehovah-Shalom:

> So Gideon built an altar there to the Lord, and called it The-Lord-Is-Peace. To this day it is still in Ophrah of the Abiezrites.
> —Judges 6:24

Christ comes to drive evil beasts (demons) out of our lives.

> I will make a covenant of peace [shalom] with them, and
> cause wild beasts to cease from the land; and they will
> dwell safely in the wilderness and sleep in the woods.
>
> —EZEKIEL 34:25

Because of Jesus we have been spiritually grafted in to the lineage of Abraham and can claim every covenantal promise in the Bible for our families. As you go through this book, I am going to lead you in declarations of the various benefits of being in covenant with God. Claim each one with strength and authority, knowing that in faith every one of God's promises to you and your family is yes and amen (2 Cor. 1:20). Jesus came so that through Him you and your seed would have access to the blessings of Abraham. So do not doubt that these are for you and your family. If you are in Christ, you are in covenant with God. You are heir to the covenant blessings of Abraham. It is very important that you and your family receive the revelation of covenant. Let's start now by declaring God's covenant blessings over your family.

DECLARE GOD'S COVENANTAL BLESSINGS OVER YOUR FAMILY

My family will not be cut off (Num. 4:18).

My family will live and not die when we come near most holy things (Num. 4:19).

My family will share the inheritance of the tribe of Judah (Josh. 15:20).

My family, like the families of Issachar, is full of mighty men of valor (1 Chron. 7:5).

The Lord will be with my family (Gen. 31:3)

Let the inheritance of the Lord come upon my family as it did upon the tribes of Israel (Josh. 13; 19).

The Lord will greatly increase the houses of the fathers in my family (1 Chron. 4:38).

My family will give glory and strength to the Lord (1 Chron. 16:28).

The Lord sets the poor in my family on high and far from affliction, and makes their families like a flock (Ps. 107:41).

My family hears the word of the Lord (Jer. 2:4).

The Lord will take my family in the night and wash their stripes and they will be baptized (Acts 16:33).

My family is blessed (Gen. 12:3).

The Lord will bless those who bless my family and curse those who curse my family (Gen. 12:3).

My family will serve in the tabernacle of God (Num. 4).

My family will multiply and increase like the tribe of Judah (1 Chron. 4:27).

The ark of the presence of the Lord dwells with my family (1 Chron. 13:14).

The blessings of the Lord are upon the households in my family (1 Chron. 13:14).

My family worships before the Lord (Ps. 22:27).

The solitary ones in my family will be brought back. Those who are bound will be brought into prosperity (Ps. 68:6).

The Lord will be God over my family, and we will be His people (Jer. 24:7).

My family will not be seduced and sold by witches and harlots, in the name of Jesus (Nah. 3:4).

My family are the sons of prophets and of the covenant God made with Abraham (Acts 3:25).

The seed of my family will be blessed (Acts 3:25).

We are a family of high priests (Acts 4:6).

The word of salvation has been sent to my family (Acts 13:26).

The Lord will send angels to accompany my family (Gen. 24:40).

The Lord will prosper my family's way (Gen. 24:40).

The descendants of my family will spread out like the dust of the earth, and we will be blessed (Gen. 28:14).

The Lord will deal well with my family (Gen. 32:9).

The Lord will bring my family out of the bondage of Egypt (Exod. 6:13).

My family strengthens the kingdom, because they walk in the way of David and Solomon (2 Chron. 11:17).

The Lord will set my family at their throne, at the entrance of Jerusalem and the cities of Judah (Jer. 1:15).

The Lord is married to my family and will bring us to Zion (Jer. 3:14).

My family will never be like the Gentiles, who serve wood and stone (Ezek. 20:32).

Let there not be any among my family who will turn their heart from the Lord our God (Deut. 29:18).

Let there be no root in my family bearing bitterness or wormwood (Deut. 29:18).

2

GOD VISITS FAMILIES

*Blessed is the Lord God of Israel, for He has
visited and redeemed His people.*

—LUKE 1:68

OD CAN VISIT individuals, and God can visit families. God's visitation brings great blessings and favor. As God's new covenant people, we can pray for and expect God to visit our family members. The word *visited* is the Greek word *episkeptomai*. It means "to look upon in order to help or to benefit, to look after, have care for, provide for: of God."[1] *Visit* also means "to go to and stay with (a person or family) or at (a place) for a short time for reasons of sociability, politeness, business, curiosity."[2] What a privilege to have the God of the universe visit us. There are many families and communities that need a visitation.

When God visits His people, He does it in a special way with a specific purpose in mind. Visitation from the Lord brings a time of refreshing. Israel missed the appointed time of their visitation (Luke 19:44). A visitation from the Lord is an appointed time—a specific time God has designated to come to His people and help them and refresh them. Acts 3:19 says, "Repent, then, and turn to God, so that your sins may be wiped out, that times of refreshing may come from the Lord" (NIV). The word translated "times" in this verse is *kairos*. It means "appointed time, an opportune time, a season"—not just time chronologically marked off on a clock or calendar. This was a time for God to converge with His people.

This is not some visit that we can conjure up, invoke, or stir up. Visitation from God is the result of covenant. It is not dependent

19

on what we do or don't do; it is dependent upon us being in covenant with God. We should ask for and believe God to visit our
family members. He will do it at the appointed time.

There are several reasons why God comes to visit with His
people:

- To bring them out of bondage
- To bring deliverance
- To bring salvation (Ps. 106:4)
- To execute judgment (Jer. 15:15)
- To impart new life (1 Sam. 2:21)
- To refresh us in the Holy Spirit (Ps. 65:9; Isa.
  59:21)
- To manifest His covenant

God promised Abraham that He would visit his descendants
and bring them out of bondage. The Book of Exodus is the fulfillment of this promise. God visited Israel because of covenant.

The visitation of God brought deliverance to Israel. The visitation brought signs and wonders. The visitation meant God sent
Moses as a deliverer. His visitation meant judgment upon Pharaoh
and the Egyptians.

Joseph believed in God's visitation. He understood the covenant
God had made with his fathers: "And Joseph said to his brethren,
'I am dying; but God will surely visit you, and bring you out of
this land to the land of which He swore to Abraham, to Isaac, and
to Jacob.'" (Gen. 50:24). This again reveals the power of covenant.
Our God is a covenant-keeping God, and we can believe in His
promises.

Joseph knew that Israel would come out of Egypt. He knew

the Lord would bring his people out of bondage and gave them instruction concerning his bones at his death (Heb. 11:22). Joseph had faith in the covenant promises of God.

Moses was sent into Egypt to announce God's visitation. The Lord told him to "go, and gather the elders of Israel together, and say unto them, The LORD God of your fathers, the God of Abraham, of Isaac, and of Jacob, appeared unto me, saying, I have surely visited you, and seen that which is done to you in Egypt" (Exod. 3:16, KJV).

God was visiting Israel in Egypt to bring them out of bondage. This visitation would result in great signs and wonders being performed through Moses. Israel experienced the supernatural intervention of God. God remembered His covenant to Abraham and promised Abraham He would bring Israel out of bondage.

There may be members in your family who are in bondage. God's supernatural intervention can occur in their lives through His visitation. It does not matter how long they have been in bondage, God can and will bring them out. There is nothing impossible with God.

The Hebrews believed the word of Moses and worshipped.

> So the people believed; and when they heard that the LORD had visited the children of Israel and that He had looked on their affliction, then they bowed their heads and worshiped.
>
> —EXODUS 4:31

They had waited for more than four hundred years for this visitation. This is everlasting power of covenant. Their enemies became God's enemies. God will do the same for your family. No matter how long it takes, His covenant will be established in the households of His covenant people.

J. I. Packer has said that a visitation of God is revival.

A visitation of God...brings to life Christians who have been sleeping and restores a deep sense of God's near presence and holiness. Thence springs a vivid sense of sin and a profound exercise of heart in repentance, praise, and love, with an evangelistic outflow.

Each revival movement has its own distinctive features, but the pattern is the same every time.

First God comes....Revival always begins with a restoration of the sense of the closeness of the Holy One.

Second, the gospel is loved as never before. The sense of God's nearness creates an overwhelming awareness of one's own sins and sinfulness, and so the power of the cleansing blood of Christ is greatly appreciated.

Then repentance deepens. In the Ulster revival in the 1920s shipyard workers brought back so many stolen tools that new sheds had to be built to house the recovered property! Repentance results in restitution.

Finally, the Spirit works fast: godliness multiplies, Christians mature, converts appear. Paul was at Thessalonica for less than three weeks, but God worked quickly and Paul left a virile church behind him.[3]

We should hunger for our families to be visited by God. It should be our desire for our families to experience the nearness of God, the closeness of His presence. This is important for life and health and strength of God's people. The growth of the kingdom is also a key benefit of a visitation from God.

THE VISITATION OF CHRIST

The arrival of Christ was a visitation. His visited Israel to redeem them and to bless them. Luke 1:68–79 records the word of the

Lord that came to Israel upon the arrival of Christ. These are the benefits of the visitation of Christ:

- Redemption
- Salvation
- Salvation from enemies
- Mercy
- Remembrance of the holy covenant
- Serve the Lord without fear
- Remission of sin
- Light
- Guidance
- Peace

Jesus came to redeem Israel from sin and their enemy, Satan. His redemption was extended to the natural and spiritual seed of Abraham.

The Gospels record the results of God's visitation. The sick were healed. The bound were delivered. The dead were raised. The blind eyes were opened. The deaf ears were unstopped. The lame walked. Demons were cast out. The oppressed were set free. There was a great release of God's power and authority on behalf of His people. Jesus became the manifestation of the covenant.

> Through the tender mercy of our God, with which the Dayspring from on high has visited us.
>
> —LUKE 1:78

The visitation of God is His tender mercy. God's mercy was manifested toward Israel, and His mercy can be manifested to your family because you are now grafted in to His new covenant through His Son, Jesus Christ. Mercy is a part of covenant. Covenant mercy is a powerful force that brings healing and deliverance.

God's visitation causes the dayspring to arise in our lives. The dayspring brings light in the midst of darkness. God's light can shine in your family. Those members of your family who are in darkness will see the light.

Miracles Happen During Visitation

You can believe God to visit your family with miracles. Family members can have an encounter with the power and authority of heaven. If you look in your Bible and focus on the stories of those who walked with God, miracles followed them everywhere. From Moses and Aaron, to Elijah and Elisha, Gideon, Joshua, to Jesus and the apostles, the evidence and visitation of God were manifested through them by miracles, signs, and wonders. In Luke 7:15–17 we find an example of this:

> So he who was dead sat up and began to speak. And He presented him to his mother. Then fear came upon all, and they glorified God, saying, "A great prophet has risen up among us"; and, "God has visited His people." And this report about Him went throughout all Judea and all the surrounding region.

The dead child was raised, causing people to glorify God. The rumor of Christ went throughout the entire region. God's visitation causes the message of Christ to spread. The salvation of families will cause the message of Christ to spread throughout communities. Many receive miracles as a result of visitation. This can happen in your household as well.

According to Psalm 8:4 God is mindful of you, and He is mindful of your family and your loved ones. God visits us because He is mindful of us. This caused the psalmist great wonder. Why would God be so mindful of man? Why would God take the time to visit us?

God is always mindful of His covenant people. God is always mindful of His covenant promises. God does visit His people with miracles to bless them, to give them an abundant life, to make His glory shine forth in the earth, and to demonstrate His great love toward us.

Ask God to visit and water your life. Ask God to visit and water your family.

> You visit the earth and water it, You greatly enrich it; the river of God is full of water; You provide their grain, for so You have prepared it. You water its ridges abundantly, You settle its furrows; You make it soft with showers, You bless its growth.
>
> —PSALM 65:9–10

God will enrich your family with His river. The river of God brings provision, healing, deliverance, joy, and blessing. The river of God brings life. Ask God to visit and refresh your family.

GOD'S VISITATION BRINGS SALVATION

> Remember me, O LORD, with the favor You have toward Your people. Oh, visit me with Your salvation.
>
> —PSALM 106:4

There may be members of your family who need a visitation that brings salvation. The favor of God is a part of the covenant. God can favor our families with salvation.

Don't let your family be like the people of Jerusalem. They missed the time of visitation.

> For days will come upon you when your enemies will build an embankment around you, surround you and close you in on every side, and level you, and your children within you, to the ground; and they will not leave in you one stone upon another, because you did not know the time of your visitation.
>
> —Luke 19:43–44

This is one of the saddest verses in Scripture. Jesus wept over the city because they missed the season of blessing and salvation. From chapter 1 you can now see the devastation of this missed appointment with God. Salvation means so much to a people. To miss the visitation of salvation is utter destruction. Because Israel rejected the visitation of salvation, God began to visit the Gentiles after He visited Israel.

> Simon has declared how God at the first visited the Gentiles to take out of them a people for His name.
>
> —Acts 15:14

Notice God visited His covenant people first, and then He visited the Gentiles. The Book of Acts records this visitation. The visitation began in the household of Cornelius. In other words, God visited a family with salvation. We will explore household salvation further in the next chapter.

Pray for your family and family members not to miss the time of visitation. Declare that they will know the appointed time for the visitation of the Lord and will have their hearts prepared to receive Him. Visitation is an important time that should not be missed. Those who miss the time of visitation miss their season of opportunity and blessing.

DECLARE THE VISITATION OF THE LORD OVER YOUR FAMILY

The Lord will visit my family and do for us as He has spoken (Gen. 21:1).

The Lord will visit the households in my family every morning (Job 7:18).

The Lord is mindful of my family and visits us (Ps. 8:4).

The Lord has visited and redeemed my family (Luke 1:68).

Through His tender mercy the Dayspring on high has visited my family (Luke 1:78).

The Lord will remember my family with favor and will visit us with His salvation (Ps. 106:4).

The Lord visited my family and has taken us as a people for Him name (Acts 15:14).

God will surely visit my family (Gen. 50:25).

The Lord has visited my family and looked upon our affliction (Exod. 4:31).

The Lord has visited my family by giving us bread (Ruth 1:6).

The Lord has tested the heart of my family. He has visited us in the night. He has tried us and found nothing. We have purposed that our mouths will not transgress (Ps. 17:3).

The Lord has visited my family, and He has watered us like the earth, greatly enriched us, and provided our grain (Ps. 65:9).

The Lord will look down from heaven and see. He will visit the vine of my family (Ps. 80:14).

The Lord will surely visit my family and bring us into the land that He swore to Abraham, Isaac, and Jacob (Gen. 50:24).

Let the Lord visit the barren women in my family that they may conceive and bear children (1 Sam. 2:21).

The Lord will remember my family. He will visit us and take vengeance for us on our persecutors (Jer. 15:15).

The Lord will visit my family and perform His good word toward us (Jer. 29:10).

The Lord will visit my family, His flock, and will make us as His royal horse in the battle (Zech. 10:3).

God has visited my family through His prophets (Luke 7:16).

Let my family know the time of the Lord's visitation (Luke 19:44).

The Lord has visited my family and has seen what has been done to us in Egypt (Exod. 3:16).

The Lord will visit my family, and we will all dwell safely (Ezek. 38:8).

3

A LAMB FOR A HOUSE

Speak to all the congregation of Israel, saying: "On the tenth of
this month every man shall take for himself a lamb, according
to the house of his father, a lamb for a household."

—EXODUS 12:3

A S I MENTIONED before, God works through families to expand His kingdom. Families are His design. Families represent His heart for relationship. God is not interested in individuals only; He is also interested in making His covenant with families just as He did with Abraham and his family. This is why He made it so that the believing person in a family unit would be the door through which His salvation could enter.

This is first seen in the Old Testament. When the death angel was on its way to kill the firstborn of every household in Egypt, the Lord instructed one person from every family to take a lamb and smear its blood over the doorpost so that their family would not see death. The same is true in the Spirit. Now you as a covenant believer—one who has been covered by the blood of the Lamb of God—can be the one through which salvation is delivered to your family. Through you, your whole household can be protected from destruction.

> Then Moses called for all the elders of Israel and said unto them, "Pick out and take lambs for yourselves according to your families, and kill the Passover lamb."
> —EXODUS 12:21

GOD'S COVENANT STARTS WITH ONE
AND EXTENDS TO THE SEED

On the same day the LORD made a covenant with Abram,
saying: "To your descendants I have given this land, from
the river of Egypt to the great river, the River Euphrates."

—GENESIS 15:18

And I will make My covenant between Me and you, and
will multiply you exceedingly

—GENESIS 17:2

So God heard their groaning, and God remembered His
covenant with Abraham, with Isaac, and with Jacob.

—EXODUS 2:24

God responded to Israel's groaning because of His covenant with
Abraham. Deliverance to the family of Abraham came because of
covenant. God will also respond to your prayers for your family
because of His covenant with you.

. . . (for the LORD your God is a merciful God), He will
not forsake you nor destroy you, nor forget the covenant
of your fathers which He swore to them.

—DEUTERONOMY 4:31

"As for Me," says the LORD, "this is My covenant with
them: My Spirit who is upon you, and My words which
I have put in your mouth, shall not depart from your
mouth, nor from the mouth of your descendants, nor
from the mouth of your descendants' descendants," says
the LORD, "from this time and forevermore."

—ISAIAH 59:21

> For I, the LORD, love justice; I hate robbery for burnt
> offering; I will direct their work in truth, and will make
> with them an everlasting covenant.
>
> —ISAIAH 61:8

God's covenant with Abraham would bring blessing to his family and to the families of the earth. Abraham was commanded to circumcise his seed in order to bring them into covenant. God eventually entered into another covenant with Abraham's seed at Sinai. The Sinai covenant included blessings and curses.

> I will bless those who bless you, and I will curse him who
> curses you; and in you all the families of the earth shall
> be blessed.
>
> —GENESIS 12:3

> Also your descendants shall be as the dust of the earth;
> you shall spread abroad to the west and the east, to the
> north and the south; and in you and in your seed all the
> families of the earth shall be blessed.
>
> —GENESIS 28:14

> A man who has friends must himself be friendly, but
> there is a friend who sticks closer than a brother.
>
> —PROVERBS 18:24

God's blessing upon a family through covenant can be seen through the life of Abraham. Abraham was called the friend of God. God entered in a blood covenant with Abraham and his seed. This is why circumcision, the sign of the covenant, included the shedding of blood. Abraham was God's covenant friend.

The two participants in the cutting of the covenant are called "covenant heads." The covenant remains in effect until both covenant heads die. If one covenant head dies, the other will extend the benefits and blessings of the covenant to the family of the deceased covenant head. In essence a blood covenant not only joins the two covenant heads together but also joins the families as well. These facts should be kept firmly in mind as we explore the reality of our redemption in the new covenant in Christ's blood.

At the conclusion of the ceremony, the two covenant heads are called "friends." The word *friend* is a covenant term that has completely lost its meaning in today's English language. The word *friend* as used in Proverbs 18:24 (quoted above) meant "covenant friend" or "blood brother." It implied the union of two people in a blood covenant.

Covenant friendship is a sacred friendship between two people resulting in each one's pledge of loyalty and complete trust. To betray covenant brought the penalty of death. Covenant friends pledge to protect each other and their families. The enemies of your friend became your enemies.

God's friendship with Abraham meant He would bless Abraham's descendants. Abraham's seed (family) would become the beneficiaries of God's mercy, favor, and compassion.

> And the LORD was gracious unto them, and had compassion on them, and regarded them, because of his covenant with Abraham, Isaac, and Jacob, and would not destroy them or cast them from His presence.
>
> —2 Kings 13:23

God's grace and compassion on Israel was a result of God's covenant with Abraham. This shows the power of covenant, and the power of covenant friendship.

God never forgot His promises to Abraham. His covenant with Abraham required Him to keep these promises.

> For He remembered His holy promise, and Abraham his
> servant.
>
> —PSALM 105:42

God referred to His covenant people as the seed of Abraham. They were Abraham's family.

> O seed of Abraham His servant, you children of Jacob,
> His chosen ones!
>
> —PSALM 105:6

The people of God would always refer back to the covenant God made with Abraham. We see it in Psalm 105:9: "...which covenant he made with Abraham, and his oath unto Isaac" (KJV). It was the foundation of their blessings and redemption.

THROUGH JESUS WE (AND OUR FAMILIES) ARE THE SEED OF ABRAHAM

> The book of the genealogy of Jesus Christ, the Son of
> David, the Son of Abraham.
>
> —MATTHEW 1:1

Jesus is the son of Abraham. Jesus is the true seed of Abraham. It was to Abraham and his seed (Christ) that the promises were made. You can see that the promises of salvation and redemption have their foundation in the covenant with Abraham.

Abraham would be the father of many nations. Abraham's seed would not only be the physical seed but also those who have the faith of Abraham. We are now Abraham's seed by faith in Jesus Christ.

The seed of Abraham entered into covenant with God at Sinai. We now enter into covenant through faith in Christ. We are now circumcised in the heart. The blessing of Abraham now comes upon all families of the earth through faith in Jesus Christ.

OPENING THE DOORS TO
SALVATION IN YOUR FAMILY

> Meanwhile praying also for us, that God would open to us a door for the word, to speak the mystery of Christ, for which I am also in chains.
>
> —COLOSSIANS 4:3

Doors are entry points that provide access. God's access into a family can come through one person. Every person is connected to someone else, and everyone has some influence in another's life. Families consist of strong interpersonal relationships that God uses to connect people to the gospel and salvation.

Throughout the New Testament the words *save*, *saved*, and *salvation* have their root in the Greek *sozo*, which means to save, to rescue, to deliver, to protect. *Sozo* is also translated in the New Testament with the words to heal, preserve, save, do well, and to make whole. The Greek *soteria* (which has its origin in *sozo*) is the main word translated "salvation." *Soteria* is also translated to deliver, health, salvation, save, and saving.

Sozo, which is used one hundred ten times in the New Testament, is originally a Greek word meaning, "to save or make well or whole." According to the Strong's *sozo* also means, "to save, deliver, heal preserve." The writers of the New Testament showed the completeness of the word *sozo* by using it in different contexts to refer to each aspect of salvation.

1. To save, keep safe and sound, to rescue one from danger or destruction (from injury or peril)

2. To save a suffering one (from perishing), i.e. one suffering from disease, to make well, heal, restore to health

3. To preserve one who is in danger of destruction, to save or rescue

4. To save in the technical biblical sense

5. To deliver from the penalties of the Messianic judgment

6. To save from the evils that obstruct the reception of the Messianic deliverance

A covenant believer can open the doors of salvation to his or her family by walking with God the way Abraham did. A covenant believer can walk in obedience and faith. A covenant believer can intercede on his family's behalf and expect God to heal and deliver. God hears the prayers of the righteous. He is friends with the faithful. The full measure of salvation is extended to your family because of covenant.

BIBLICAL EXAMPLES OF SALVATION COMING TO HOUSEHOLDS

The Bible has many examples of salvation coming to households. The first example I will give the household of Cornelius. God chose Cornelius and his house to begin His work of salvation among the Gentiles.

> And the following day they entered Caesarea. Now Cornelius was waiting for them, and had called together his relatives and close friends.
>
> —ACTS 10:24

Cornelius called his kinsmen and friends together to hear what Peter had to say. This is an example of how one person can be the door through which the gospel comes to family and friends. We see this principle throughout Scripture. Households are blessed with salvation through the gospel. The next example is the Philippian jailer.

> But at midnight Paul and Silas were praying and singing hymns to God, and the prisoners were listening to them. Suddenly there was a great earthquake, so that the foundations of the prison were shaken; and immediately all the doors were opened and everyone's chains were loosed. And the keeper of the prison, awaking from sleep and seeing the prison doors open, supposing the prisoners had fled, drew his sword and was about to kill himself. But Paul called with a loud voice, saying, "Do yourself no harm, for we are all here."
>
> Then he called for a light, ran in, and fell down trembling before Paul and Silas. And he brought them out and said, "Sirs, what must I do to be saved?"
>
> So they said, "Believe on the Lord Jesus Christ, and you will be saved, you and your household." Then they spoke the word of the Lord to him and to all who were in his house. And he took them the same hour of the night and washed their stripes. And immediately he and all his family were baptized.
>
> —Acts 16:25–33

The word of the Lord came to the keeper of the prison and his house. His entire house received the word of the Lord and were baptized. Notice the words of Paul, "Thou shalt be saved, and thy house" (KJV). Paul understood that the jailer was an opening for the entire household. We often think in terms of individuals in the West, but the biblical worldview looks at the house. This is the power of the family, especially when the head of the family accepts Christ.

Paul baptized the house of Stephanas.

> Yes, I also baptized the household of Stephanas. Besides, I do not know whether I baptized any other.
>
> —1 CORINTHIANS 1:16

The household of Lydia was baptized.

> And when she and her household were baptized, she begged us, saying, "If you have judged me to be faithful to the Lord, come to my house and stay." So she persuaded us.
>
> —ACTS 16:15

The household of Narcissus was in the Lord.

> Greet Herodion, my countryman. Greet those who are of the household of Narcissus who are in the Lord.
>
> —ROMANS 16:11

The household of Crispus received salvation:

> Then Crispus, the ruler of the synagogue, believed on the Lord with all his household. And many of the Corinthians, hearing, believed and were baptized.
>
> —ACTS 18:8

The nobleman's house believed:

So the father knew that it was at the same hour in which
Jesus said to him, "Your son lives." And he himself
believed, and his whole household.

—JOHN 4:53

Salvation came to the house of Zaccheus:

And Jesus said to him, "Today salvation has come to this
house, because he also is a son of Abraham."

—LUKE 19:9

In the Old Testament the Lord blessed the house of Obed-
Edom and all that he had.

The ark of the LORD remained in the house of Obed-
Edom the Gittite three months. And the LORD blessed
Obed-Edom and all his household.

—2 SAMUEL 6:11

He kept the house of David on the throne and saved them from
destruction.

Yet the LORD would not destroy the house of David,
because of the covenant that He had made with David,
and since He had promised to give a lamp to him and to
his sons forever.

—2 CHRONICLES 21:7

God's love (mercy, loving-kindness) is steadfast, which means
enduring and sure. The Hebrew word for "sure mercies" is *aman*,
meaning "sure, lasting, faithful, established, firm, and reliable."

God's mercy to David was sure. David spoke of the resurrection.

He could die with the assurance that he would be resurrected through Messiah.

David's family and descendants benefited from the covenant God made with David. God's mercy prevented his family from being destroyed.

> And that He raised Him from the dead, no more to return to corruption, He has spoken thus: "I will give you the sure mercies of David."
>
> —ACTS 13:34

The mercy upon David's house was sure. The steadfast love of God was manifested from generation to generation.

Rahab the harlot is an example of faith, and she believed for her deliverance and the deliverance of her household.

> By faith the harlot Rahab did not perish with those who did not believe, when she had received the spies with peace.
>
> —HEBREWS 11:31

Rahab is one of the greatest examples in Scripture of someone's faith saving their house. Rahab's faith saved her and her house. It is important for believers to intercede and believe God for the salvation of their families.

Noah prepared an ark for the saving of his house. Noah's entire family was saved through the flood because of Noah's obedience.

> By faith Noah, being divinely warned of things not yet seen, moved with godly fear, prepared an ark for the saving of his household, by which he condemned the world and became heir of the righteousness which is according to faith.
>
> —HEBREWS 11:7

The obedience of a family member will affect the entire family.

These are numerous examples in Scripture of salvation coming to a household. This has been seen throughout history with God's Word coming to countless households. Only eternity will reveal the number of households that have been saved over generations. The good news is that God desires to visit and save your household as well.

> But whatever house you enter, first say, "Peace to this house." And if a son of peace is there, your peace will rest on it; if not, it will return to you.
>
> —LUKE 10:5–6

Shalom (peace) can come to a house. The gospel is the gospel of peace. Salvation brings peace. Peace is the word *shalom*, meaning health, favor, and wholeness. This is God's desire for households that believe the gospel of peace.

COVENANT HOUSEHOLDS SUPPORT KINGDOM MINISTRIES

> The Lord grant mercy to the household of Onesiphorus, for he often refreshed me, and was not ashamed of my chain.
>
> —2 TIMOTHY 1:16

> Greet Prisca and Aquila, and the household of Onesiphorus.
>
> —2 TIMOTHY 4:19

Paul mentioned the house of Onesiphorus. He saluted this house in his letters. This house evidently was special to Paul. Ministers need families that support and bless them in ministry. The house of Onesiphorus refreshed Paul and was not ashamed of his chains. Households can be a blessing to ministers and help advance the kingdom of God.

Paul mentioned other households in his letters, including his kinsman Herodion:

> Greet Apelles, approved in Christ. Greet those who are of the household of Aristobulus.
>
> —ROMANS 16:10

> Greet Herodion, my countryman. Greet those who are of the household of Narcissus who are in the Lord.
>
> —ROMANS 16:11

COVENANT PROMISE FOR THE SALVATION OF YOUR CHILDREN

> But thus says the LORD: "Even the captives of the mighty shall be taken away, and the prey of the terrible be delivered; for I will contend with him who contends with you, and I will save your children."
>
> —ISAIAH 49:25

This was God's promise to His covenant people. We are now the seed of Abraham by faith, and we can claim this promise for our children.

Fragmented families can be a hindrance to salvation coming to families. There are many families that are divided and filled with strained relationships. We must pray for healing, forgiveness, and restoration to come to families. The breakdown of the family is epidemic in some places. It is the will of God to turn the hearts of families.

And he will turn the hearts of the fathers to the children,
and the hearts of the children to their fathers, lest I come
and strike the earth with a curse.

—MALACHI 4:6

It should not be unusual for entire families to come to salvation. The breakdown of the family in many cases hinders this from happening. This is why the enemy seeks to destroy families, and as a result hinder the family members from receiving salvation.

Families are God's natural channels of communication. Through family relationships people are exposed to the Word of the Lord.

Family (household) salvations are a key to exponential growth and kingdom expansion. The covenant will have an effect on the household. The church will grow exponentially with the salvation of families.

When a person is saved, the family of that person will be impacted spiritually. The family will have a witness, and light will come into any darkness that family has been in generationally. This will be a major blow to the work of the enemy in that family and bloodline.

> "We are genetically predisposed to cling to our family," explains Dr. Bengtson. "It is wired into us the need to bond with family members. Historically, family relationships have played the most basic role of all—ensuring survival. Today, most people rely on family interactions to provide an affirming, positive experience. They provide a sense of support and an identity of who we are and what's unique about us."...
>
> People who cultivate extended family relationships are at an advantage emotionally and are often more successful in their personal lives. Both children and adults

benefit from these relationships during times of great stress, such as tragedy, death or divorce. They also reap the rewards when joyous events enter their lives, whether it is a new job, a new child or a milestone birthday.[1]

PRAYERS FOR FAMILY SALVATION

God, You are the faithful God, the covenant-keeping God. You keep covenant and loyalty to a thousand generations. I have a covenant with You through the blood of Jesus, which provides salvation, forgiveness, and blessing to my life. You promised Abraham that through his seed all families of the earth would be blessed. Jesus is the promised seed, and through Him my family can be blessed.

I come before You on the behalf of my family, and ask for Your salvation, protection, deliverance, and healing to manifest in my family. I pray for anyone in my family who is not in covenant with You to be drawn to You by Your Spirit and to accept Jesus as Lord and Savior. I pray for covenant blessing to come to my family and that my family would benefit from covenant blessings.

Have mercy upon my family, and let Your loving-kindness and tender mercy be over us. Let Your grace and favor be upon my family. Let my family in this generation be blessed, and let generations to come walk in covenant with You and be blessed.

Lord, save my family.

Lord, let Your Word come to every family member, and let them believe.

I bind and rebuke every demon that has been assigned to my family members to prevent them from receiving salvation.

Lord, let salvation come to my household.

Let my household be like the household of Obed-Edom (2 Sam. 6:11).

DECLARE THE SALVATION OF THE LORD OVER YOUR FAMILY

My family is waiting for Your salvation, O Lord (Gen. 49:18).

My family hopes for the salvation of the Lord, and we do His commandments (Ps. 119:166).

My eyes have seen the salvation of the Lord for my family (Luke 2:30).

The Lord is the rock and salvation for my family. He is our defense, and we will not be moved (Ps. 62:6).

Salvation belongs to the Lord, and His blessing is upon my family (Ps. 3:8).

My family trusts in the Lord's mercy, and our hearts rejoice in His salvation (Ps. 13:5).

My family rejoices in the Lord's salvation (Ps. 35:9).

The Lord, our salvation, makes haste to help my family (Ps. 38:22).

The Lord will restore to my family the joy of His salvation and will uphold us by His generous Spirit (Ps. 51:12).

Let the way of the Lord be made known in my family and His salvation among us all (Ps. 67:2).

The Lord works salvation in our midst (Ps. 74:12).

The Lord shows mercy to my family and grants us His salvation (Ps. 85:7).

The Lord will satisfy my family with long life, and He will show us His salvation (Ps. 91:16).

My family seeks diligently the salvation of the Lord and His righteous word (Ps. 119:123).

My family praises You, O Lord, for You have answered us and have become our salvation (Ps. 118:21).

My family longs for the salvation of the Lord, and His law is our delight (Ps. 119:174).

My family hopes and waits quietly for the salvation of the Lord (Lam. 3:26).

The Lord has risen up a horn of salvation for my family (Luke 1:69).

By the remission of their sins, the knowledge of salvation is given to my family (Luke 1:77).

The grace of God, which brings salvation, has appeared to my family (Titus 2:11).

Jesus is the author of eternal salvation for my family because we obey Him (Heb. 5:9).

God is my family's salvation. We will trust and not be afraid. The Lord is our strength and song (Isa. 12:2).

The Lord will bring His righteousness near to my family. It will not be far off. His salvation will not linger. He will place salvation in us, for we are His glory (Isa. 46:13).

Truly, the Lord our God is the salvation of my family (Jer. 3:23).

The Lord has given my family the shield of His salvation (2 Sam. 22:36).

The Lord is the rock of salvation for my family (2 Sam. 22:47).

The Lord is the tower of salvation for my family. He shows us and our descendants His mercy (2 Sam. 22:51).

My family will sing to the Lord and proclaim the good news of His salvation from day to day (1 Chron. 16:23).

My family rejoices in the Lord's salvation (Ps. 9:14).

The glory of my family is great in the salvation of the Lord. Honor and majesty have been placed upon us (Ps. 21:5).

My family waits on the Lord all the day, for He is the God of our salvation (Ps. 25:5).

The God of my family's salvation loads us daily with benefits (Ps. 68:19).

The God of our salvation will restore us and cause His anger toward us to cease (Ps. 85:4).

The Lord's salvation is near to my family, because we fear Him. His glory dwells in our land (Ps. 85:9).

The Lord has remembered His mercy and faithfulness to my family. We have seen His salvation (Ps. 98:3).

The Lord will remember my family with His favor and visit us with His salvation (Ps. 106:4).

My family will take up the cup of salvation and will call upon the name of the Lord (Ps. 116:13).

The Lord's salvation will come upon my family according to His word (Ps. 119:41).

The Lord has clothed the priests in my family with salvation (Ps. 132:16).

The Lord is the strength of our salvation. He covers our heads in the day of battle (Ps. 140:7).

The Lord takes pleasure in my family and beautifies us with His salvation (Ps. 149:4).

The Lord's salvation is about to come to my family, and His righteousness will be revealed (Isa. 56:1).

Today salvation comes to the house of my family, because we are sons of Abraham (Luke 19:9).

The salvation of God has been sent to my family, and they will hear it (Acts 28:28).

The prophets have prophesied that the grace of salvation will come to my family (1 Pet. 1:10).

In the day of salvation the Lord has helped my family (2 Cor. 6:2).

Now is the day of salvation for my family (2 Cor. 6:2).

My family smiles at their enemies because they rejoice in the salvation of the Lord (1 Sam. 2:1).

Today the Lord has accomplished salvation in my family (1 Sam. 11:13).

The Lord is the shield and horn of salvation for my family. He saves us from violence (2 Sam. 22:3).

Although my family is not so with God, He has made us an everlasting covenant. This is our salvation, and He will make it increase (2 Sam. 23:5).

The Lord will increase the salvation of my family (2 Sam. 23:5).

My family glorifies the Lord and orders their conduct aright; therefore He will show us His salvation (Ps. 50:23).

The Lord is salvation for my family in the time of trouble (Isa. 33:2).

My family will be saved with an everlasting salvation, and we will not be ashamed or disgraced (Isa. 45:17).

The Lord's salvation for my family is from generation to generation (Isa. 51:8).

The gospel of Christ is the power of salvation to my family (Rom. 1:16).

It is high time for my family to awake out of sleep, for now our salvation is nearer than when we first believed (Rom. 13:11).

May godly sorrow produce repentance in my family, leading them to salvation (2 Cor. 7:10).

My family trusts the Lord, after hearing the word of truth, the gospel of our salvation. We are sealed with the Holy Spirit of promise (Eph. 1:13).

My family will stand still and see the salvation of the Lord, which He will accomplish today (Exod. 14:13).

God of our salvation will save my family. He will gather us together and deliver us to give thanks to His holy name, to triumph in His praise (1 Chron. 16:35).

Violence, waste, and destruction shall no longer be heard of in my family. We will call our walls salvation and our gates praise (Isa. 60:18).

The Lord has clothed my family with the garments of salvation and covered us with robes of righteousness (Isa. 61:10).

Our salvation goes forth like a lamp that burns (Isa. 62:1).

From the beginning God chose my family for salvation through sanctification by the Spirit and belief in the truth (2 Thess. 2:13).

My family will not need to fight this battle. We will position ourselves, stand still, and see the salvation of the Lord, who is with us (2 Chron. 20:17).

The Lord has, in an acceptable time, heard my family. In the day of salvation He has helped us. The Lord will preserve us, restore us, and cause us to inherit the desolate heritages (Isa. 49:8).

How beautiful are the feet of my family, who bring good news, peace, and glad tidings of good things, who proclaim salvation (Isa. 52:7).

Salvation, strength, the kingdom of God, and the power of Christ have come to my family. Our accuser has been cast down (Rev. 12:10).

DELIVERANCE AND
HEALING FOR FAMILIES

*Believe on the Lord Jesus Christ, and you will be saved
[healed and delivered], you and your household.*

—ACTS 16:31

A DEEPER UNDERSTANDING OF the word *salvation* helps us to know that in Christ we can also expect healing and deliverance for our families. As we walk in covenant with God, we open the door for the blood of Christ to flow into our family lines and break the bonds and chains of demonic oppression and possession off of our family members. When one person in a family comes to Christ and lines up with the new covenant, they have activated the promise of God for their whole family to be saved, healed, and delivered.

The late Cecil J. duCille says:

> Many of us might wonder why it is that when God begins to work in a family, many of its members get saved one after the other. The answer is very simple. Satan's kingdom is set up under different principalities, which consists of princes each with their own areas of rule. These princes further divide people into many categories, but the most important one is the family category. Every family is adopted by devils, or agents of Satan. These are called "family spirits," or "familiar spirits." They live and feed upon families so long that their traits are regarded by most families as just family traits. And so they are not

even recognized by most of us as being demonic qualities. We would even boast of them as being our qualities.
In my family we used to boast of our prowess in fighting.
We would proudly look back upon our ancestry as being
mighty warriors, when in truth and in fact, they were
demon-possessed. Even the pride, which I find in families
and nations, is nothing but demonic pride. Most of it has
no real grounds; most of it (that we glory in) is what we
should be ashamed of.

The first thing that happens when Jesus Christ comes
into one's life is that this satanic family possession is hit
by the blood of Jesus Christ. Many of these spirits, which
may have oppressed one's family for ages, have not only
been blasted by the blood of Jesus, but have been put out
of action forever and cast into the abyss, from whence
they will not return until Jesus comes to judge the quick
and the dead. From this understanding, we can see then
why it is that when one person in a family is saved, the
whole family begins to be released. The battle does not
stop there, but it goes on and on. With every victory that
one wins over his basic Adamic nature, he is firing a dart
or throwing bombs at Satan on behalf of his family.[1]

LEPROSY IN THE HOUSE

And the LORD spoke to Moses and Aaron, saying: "When
you have come into the land of Canaan, which I give you
as a possession, and I put the leprous plague in a house in
the land of your possession, and he who owns the house
comes and tells the priest, saying, 'It seems to me that
there is some plague in the house,' then the priest shall
command that they empty the house, before the priest
goes into it to examine the plague, that all that is in the

house may not be made unclean; and afterward the priest shall go in to examine the house. And he shall examine the plague; and indeed if the plague is on the walls of the house with ingrained streaks, greenish or reddish, which appear to be deep in the wall, then the priest shall go out of the house, to the door of the house, and shut up the house seven days. And the priest shall come again on the seventh day and look; and indeed if the plague has spread on the walls of the house, then the priest shall command that they take away the stones in which is the plague, and they shall cast them into an unclean place outside the city. And he shall cause the house to be scraped inside, all around, and the dust that they scrape off they shall pour out in an unclean place outside the city. Then they shall take other stones and put them in the place of those stones, and he shall take other mortar and plaster the house.

"Now if the plague comes back and breaks out in the house, after he has taken away the stones, after he has scraped the house, and after it is plastered, then the priest shall come and look; and indeed if the plague has spread in the house, it is an active leprosy in the house. It is unclean."

—LEVITICUS 14:33–44

Leprosy is a type of sin. God gave specific instructions to the priests when they found a plague of leprosy in the house. Jesus came to cleanse lepers. Many individual lepers were cleansed. Leprosy can also be in families.

If leprosy was found in a house, it was considered unclean. The house would then be burned with fire. Jesus can cleanse our families from sin and deliver our families from unclean spirits. The

Holy Spirit is that fire that will burn the spiritual leprosy in our families.

Salvation is also deliverance from sickness and demons. People brought their children to Jesus for deliverance. This was the covenant right of Israel.

A father brought his son to Jesus for deliverance.

> Lord, have mercy on my son, for he is an epileptic and suffers severely; for he often falls into the fire and often into the water.
>
> —Matthew 17:15

A Gentile woman came to Jesus on the behalf of her daughter.

> And behold, a woman of Canaan came from that region and cried out to Him, saying, "Have mercy on me, O Lord, Son of David! My daughter is severely demon-possessed."
>
> —Matthew 15:22

The woman of Canaan had no covenant right to healing for her daughter, but she received because of her faith. This shows the power of faith. Many who had a covenant right did not receive because of unbelief, and those without a covenant right received because of their faith.

Multitudes brought their loved ones to Jesus for healing and deliverance. Many of the miracles of healing and deliverance occurred in the ministry of Christ as people brought their loved ones and friends to him. Matthew, Mark, and Luke record these miracles.

This is Luke's account. Those vexed with unclean spirits were healed.

> And He came down with them and stood on a level place with a crowd of His disciples and a great multitude of people from all Judea and Jerusalem, and from the seacoast of Tyre and Sidon, who came to hear Him and be healed of their diseases, as well as those who were tormented with unclean spirits. And they were healed. And the whole multitude sought to touch Him, for power went out from Him and healed them all.
>
> —Luke 6:17–19

This is Matthew's account. Those possessed with devils and tormented were healed.

> Then His fame went throughout all Syria; and they brought to Him all sick people who were afflicted with various diseases and torments, and those who were demon-possessed, epileptics, and paralytics; and He healed them. Great multitudes followed Him—from Galilee, and from Decapolis, Jerusalem, Judea, and beyond the Jordan.
>
> —Matthew 4:24–25

This is Mark's account. Those with unclean spirits were healed.

> And a great multitude from Galilee followed Him, and from Judea and Jerusalem and Idumea and beyond the Jordan; and those from Tyre and Sidon, a great multitude, when they heard how many things He was doing, came to Him. So He told His disciples that a small boat should be kept ready for Him because of the multitude, lest they should crush Him. For He healed many, so that as many as had afflictions pressed about Him to touch Him. And the unclean spirits, whenever they saw Him,

fell down before Him and cried out, saying, "You are the Son of God."

—MARK 3:7–11

God's covenant positions you and your family for miracles, including healing and deliverance.

The same thing happened through the apostles.

> They brought the sick out into the streets and laid them on beds and couches, that at least the shadow of Peter passing by might fall on some of them. Also a multitude gathered from the surrounding cities to Jerusalem, bringing sick people and those who were tormented by unclean spirits, and they were all healed.
>
> —ACTS 5:15–16

Bring your loved ones to the Lord for healing and deliverance. We have seen many family members brought for prayer by believing loved ones receive healing and deliverance. This reveals the power of the family unit and covenant relationships.

This was duplicated in every village and city that Jesus entered into. People brought their sick loved ones to touch the border of His garment.

> Wherever He entered, into villages, cities, or the country, they laid the sick in the marketplaces, and begged Him that they might just touch the hem of His garment. And as many as touched Him were made well.
>
> —MARK 6:56

Those who touched Christ were made whole. People brought their loved ones to Christ for healing and deliverance. Bring your loved ones to the Lord and watch God perform miracles on their behalf.

YOUR FAITH WILL RELEASE HEALING POWER TO YOUR LOVED ONES

> And He said to her, "Daughter, your faith has made you well. Go in peace, and be healed of your affliction."
>
> —MARK 5:34

Faith releases the healing anointing. Unbelief blocks healing. As I mentioned earlier, the main thing to having faith in the power of God to heal your family is to have a revelation of His covenant with you. When you understand covenant, you will understand that healing is for you and your family. This is something that God wants to do. By your faith you can begin to put a demand on the healing power of God.[2]

Faith is like a vacuum that draws out the anointing. Jesus not only ministered with the anointing, but He also let the people know He was anointed (Luke 4:18). When they heard He was anointed, it was their responsibility to believe and receive. The people of Nazareth did not believe and could not draw from His anointing. (See Mark 6:1–6.) He could do no mighty work in Nazareth because of their unbelief. If they would have believed, they could have drawn from His anointing and been healed.

But the woman with the issue of blood believed. She believed enough to press through the crowds, reach out, and touch the healer Himself. In Luke 8:46 Jesus says, "Somebody touched Me, for I perceived power going out from Me."

Jesus perceived that power ("virtue," KJV) had left Him. The woman drew healing power out of Him with her faith. The word *power* is the Greek word *dunamis*, which means ability, strength, or might. When you have faith that you or your loved one will be healed, you draw out the healing power of God. His power is released on their behalf. Thus, the anointing is the power of God.

> When she heard about Jesus, she came behind Him in the crowd and touched His garment.
>
> —MARK 5:27

This woman had heard of Jesus. She had heard about the healing anointing that was upon Him. She had heard that a prophet of God was ministering in Israel.

When people hear about the anointing, their faith will increase in this area, and they will then have the knowledge and faith to put a demand on the anointing. Look at what happened in the apostles' day.

> And believers were increasingly added to the Lord, mul-titudes of both men and women, so that they brought the sick out into the streets and laid them on beds and couches, that at least the shadow of Peter passing by might fall on some of them. Also a multitude gathered from the surrounding cities to Jerusalem, bringing sick people and those who were tormented by unclean spirits, and they were all healed.
>
> —ACTS 5:14–16

Here we see people coming "from the surrounding cities to Jerusalem." Where there is a demand, there is a supply. There was enough anointing available to heal *everyone*. These people put a demand on the anointing that flowed from the apostles. When people come to meetings, sometimes from long distances, and put a demand on the gift, they will receive miracles.

> Now it happened on a certain day, as He was teaching,
> that there were Pharisees and teachers of the law sitting
> by, who had come out of every town of Galilee, Judea,
> and Jerusalem. And the power of the Lord was present
> to heal them.
>
> —Luke 5:17

The word *power* here is *dunamis*, which is the same word translated as "virtue" in Luke 8:46 (kjv). The woman with the issue of blood drew virtue from the body of Jesus with her faith. So we can say that healing virtue was in the house as Jesus taught. When healing virtue (anointing) is present, we can use our faith to put a demand on that anointing. It will then be released for healing.

> Then behold, men brought on a bed a man who was para-
> lyzed, whom they sought to bring in and lay before Him.
> And when they could not find how they might bring him
> in, because of the crowd, they went up on the housetop
> and let him down with his bed through the tiling into
> the midst before Jesus. When He saw their faith, He said
> to him, "Man, your sins are forgiven you."
>
> —Luke 5:18–20

Through their faith they put a demand on the anointing present in that room. As a result, healing virtue was released and the man was healed. There are times when the presence of the Lord is thick like a cloud in a service. When the anointing is present to this degree, all we need to do is use our faith to put a demand upon it. Healing and miracles come as a result of putting a demand on the anointing.

We put a demand on the anointing with our *faith*. The Lord has given us the gift of faith for this purpose. We can expect that God will honor our faith because we are in covenant with Him. The Lord desires that we use our faith to put a demand (withdrawal) on the gifts of God, and He desires to heal us and our families.

DECLARE DELIVERANCE AND HEALING OVER YOUR FAMILY

Through the cleanliness of the hands of my family, even the guilty have been delivered (Job 22:30).

The Lord will deliver my family in their suffering and speaks to them in their affliction (Job 36:15).

The Lord will deliver my family from death and keep them alive in famine (Ps. 33:19).

The Lord will deliver my family from evildoers and save them from bloodthirsty men (Ps. 59:2).

My family cried out to the Lord in our trouble, and He delivered us from our distress (Ps. 107:6).

The Lord has delivered my family from such a deadly peril. On Him we have set our hope that He will continue to deliver us (2 Cor. 1:10).

The Lord has delivered my family from the hand of the enemy and ransomed us from the clutches of the ruthless (Job 6:23).

Our fathers put their trust in the Lord, and He delivered them (Ps. 22:4).

The Lord will deliver my family from the sword and our precious lives from the power of the dogs (Ps. 22:20).

The Lord will deliver my family from our enemies and from those who pursue us (Ps. 31:15).

The Lord delivered my family from all our fears (Ps. 34:4).

The Lord has delivered my family from the hand of the wicked (Ps. 82:4).

The Lord has delivered my family from the depths of the grave (Ps. 86:13).

The Lord has looked upon the suffering of my family and delivered us, because we have not forgotten His law (Ps. 119:153).

Our supplication came before, O God, and You delivered my family according to Your promise (Ps. 119:170).

Righteousness has delivered my family from death (Prov. 11:4).

The Lord turns toward my family and delivers us, because of His unfailing love (Ps. 6:4).

The Lord has delivered my family from the attacks of people and made us the head of nations (Ps. 18:43).

My family may have many troubles, but the Lord delivers us from them all (Ps. 34:19).

The Lord rescues my family from the mire. He will not let us sink. He will deliver us from those who hate us (Ps. 69:14).

The Lord will uphold my family with His right hand, that we who love Him may be delivered (Ps. 108:6).

The Lord will reach down His hand from on high to deliver my family and rescue us from the mighty waters (Ps. 144:7).

The Lord has delivered my family today from those who rose up against us (2 Sam. 18:31).

The Lord will deliver my family and strike all our enemies on the jaw and break the teeth of the wicked (Ps. 3:7).

The Lord brought my family up out of Egypt and delivered us from the power of Egypt and all the kingdoms that have oppressed us (1 Sam. 10:18).

The Lord God moves about the camp of my family to protect us and deliver our enemies to us. Our camp is holy. The Lord will not turn away from us (Deut. 23:14).

My family commits to the Lord and will serve Him only, and He will deliver us out of the hand of the Philistines (1 Sam. 7:3).

HEALING

The Lord forgives my family of all our iniquities and heals all our diseases (Ps. 103:3).

The Lord heals the brokenhearted in my family and binds up their wounds (Ps. 147:3).

The Lord has listened to my family and healed us (2 Chron. 30:20).

My family cried out to God, and He healed us (Ps. 30:2).

The Lord sent His word and healed my family, and He delivered us from our destructions (Ps. 107:20).

The blind and the lame of my family come to the Lord, and He will heal them (Matt. 21:14).

The demon possessed in my family are healed by the Lord (Luke 8:36).

The Lord will heal my family, and they will return to Him (Isa. 19:22).

The Lord will bring health and healing to my family and reveal to them the abundance of peace and truth (Jer. 33:6).

The Lord is merciful to my family. He heals our souls (Ps. 41:4).

By His stripes my family is healed (Isa. 53:5).

Jesus will come and heal my family (Matt. 8:7).

The Lord is moved with compassion for the great multitude in my family. He heals our sick (Matt. 14:14).

The power goes out from the Lord, and He heals all in my family (Luke 6:19).

My family is healed from this very hour (Matt. 15:28).

The Lord has healed all the females in my family, and they will bear children (Gen. 20:17).

The Lord will heal my family's backsliding, and indeed they do come (Jer. 3:22).

The Lord restores health to my family and heals us of our wounds (Jer. 30:17).

The Lord heals every sickness and every disease in my family (Matt. 9:35).

The Lord will lay hands on every one in my family and heal them (Luke 4:40).

The report of the Lord is getting around in my family, and they will come to Him to hear Him and be healed of their infirmities (Luke 5:15).

Unclean spirits will come out of many in my family who are possessed, and those who are paralyzed and lame will be healed (Acts 8:7).

My family will confess their trespasses to one another and will pray for one another and be healed (James 5:16).

The healing for my family will spring forth speedily (Isa. 58:8).

The Lord will come and lay hands on the children in my family who lie at the point of death that they may be healed and live (Matt. 5:23).

My family will diligently heed the voice of the Lord our God and do what is right in His sight, give ear to His commandments, and keep all His statutes, and He will bring none of the diseases of Egypt upon us (Exod. 15:26).

The Lord has heard the prayers of my family. He has seen our tears, and surely He will heal us (2 Kings 20:5).

The power of the Lord is present to heal my family (Luke 5:17).

5

THE COVENANTAL
MERCY OF GOD

Blessed is the Lord God of Israel, for He has visited and redeemed
His people, and has raised up a horn of salvation for us in the
house of His servant David. . . . To perform the mercy prom-
ised to our fathers and to remember His holy covenant.

—LUKE 1:68–72

THE BASIS OF the old and new covenant is God's extension of tender mercy toward His chosen people. Mercy is the covenant performed on behalf of the seed of Abraham. When God is in covenant with a person, there is always evidence of His tender mercies on their life. A lot of times when we think about mercy, we think of it in terms of forgiveness. Mercy is much more than forgiveness of sins.

Mercy is getting God's involvement on whatever you need help in. Do you need deliverance? The Lord will have mercy on you. Do you need healing? The Lord will have mercy on you. Do you need restoration in your marriage? The Lord will extend His mercy to you. Do you need breakthrough in your finances? May the Lord have mercy on you. Mercy is God acting in a covenantal way for whatever you have need of.

The Hebrew word for *mercy* is *checed*. It is translated in English as "mercy, kindness, lovingkindness, goodness, kindly, merciful, favour, good, goodliness, pity."[1] A related Hebrew word, *racham*, speaks even more closely to the covenant mercy of God. It means "to love, love deeply, have mercy, be compassionate, have tender affection, have compassion."[2]

You see it here in 2 Kings 13:23:

> But the Lord was gracious to them, had *compassion* [or mercy] on them, and regarded them, because of His covenant with Abraham, Isaac, and Jacob, and would not yet destroy them or cast them from His presence.
>
> —EMPHASIS ADDED

The word *compassion* in this verse is the same Hebrew word, *racham*, used for *mercy* in other places in the Old Testament (Exod. 33:19; Ps. 102:13; Prov. 28:13; Isa. 14:1; 30:18). The idea is that God's mercy, compassion, and pity are for His covenant people. Mercy moves God and causes Him to act. That's why the Bible says that Jesus was moved with compassion and healed the sick (Matt. 14:14).

The tender mercies, loving-kindness, and compassion of God are also seen throughout the history of Israel. Although Israel continually broke covenant, God never removed His compassion from them because of His covenant loyalty to Abraham, His covenant friend. God's mercy was continually extended to Israel through God's deliverance and preservation. God's mercy can be seen through His compassion.

A lot of times we hear in regard to covenant the judgment of the Lord coming down on covenant breakers and spiritual harlots, but God's covenant is really a covenant of mercy, loving-kindness, and compassion. It is because of God's great love and compassion that He extended His covenant to Israel.

Because you are the seed of Abraham through Christ, God will have compassion on your loved ones. God's compassion reaches the sick and demonized. God's compassion can touch individuals and families. Pray for His compassion to reach the members of your family.

> The LORD is gracious and full of compassion, slow to anger and great in mercy.
>
> —PSALM 145:8

THE WORKS OF JESUS WERE A MANIFESTATION OF THE COVENANT OF MERCY

Jesus is the greatest manifestation of God's mercy ever known to man. His incarnation was the manifestation of eternal salvation and eternal redemption. The works that Jesus performed while on earth were acts of mercy on behalf of Israel. Luke 1:68–75 identifies all that Jesus was to fulfill during His life on earth:

> Blessed is the Lord God of Israel, for He has visited and redeemed His people, and has raised up a horn of salvation for us in the house of His servant David, as He spoke by the mouth of His holy prophets, who have been since the world began, that we should be saved from our enemies and from the hand of all who hate us, *to perform the mercy promised to our fathers and to remember His holy covenant*, the oath which He swore to our father Abraham: to grant us that we, being delivered from the hand of our enemies, might serve Him without fear, in holiness and righteousness before Him all the days of our life.
>
> —EMPHASIS ADDED

Jesus came to enact His Father's covenant on behalf of Israel. He came to show them the fullness of their redemption, the revelation of the benefits of salvation, and the way to deliverance so that they would be able to worship and serve God without fear. It was God's compassion and great mercy that sent Jesus to Israel.

The works that Jesus did were the works of the Father. They were works of mercy. The miracles, signs, and wonders were a revelation of God's mercy for Israel. That is why in the Gospels we see people approach Jesus with their issues, saying, "Son of David, have mercy upon me." And Jesus was moved with compassion to heal the sick.

> And when Jesus went out He saw a great multitude; and He was moved with compassion for them, and healed their sick.
>
> —MATTHEW 14:14

- Jesus opened the eyes of the blind through compassion (Mark 10:46–52).
- Jesus cleansed the leper through compassion (Mark 1:41).
- The father brought his demonized child to Jesus for healing, and Jesus delivered his child through compassion (Mark 9:21–23).
- Jesus raised a child from the dead because of compassion and restored the son to his mother (Luke 7:12–14).

Jesus was moved with compassion when He saw the condition of the lost sheep of the house of Israel (Matt. 9:36). Jesus then sent out the twelve, and later the seventy to heal the sick and cast out devils. Jesus never ministered outside of Israel. God's covenant promises were directed to Israel, and His covenant compassion manifested through healing.

> And when He had called His twelve disciples to Him, He gave them power over unclean spirits, to cast them out, and to heal all kinds of sickness and all kinds of disease.
> —MATTHEW 10:1

The Twelve were sent out after Jesus was moved with compassion. This sending of the Twelve reveals the covenant mercy and compassion of God manifesting through the ministry of Christ. God's compassion was being shown upon the family of Abraham.

Compassion caused Christ to send out His disciples to bring healing and deliverance to the seed of Abraham. This is all based on covenant. Covenant is the framework through which compassion flows to bring healing and deliverance. If God did it for Abraham's family through covenant, then He will do it for your family through covenant.

GOD IS A GOD OF COMPASSION

God's compassion needs to be understand in a covenantal context. God's compassion can be seen in His dealings with Israel throughout their history. God continually had mercy upon them and delivered them in spite of their constant rebellion and covenant violations. The Book of Judges is an example of God's compassion upon Israel in raising up deliverers when they called upon Him.

> But He, being full of compassion, forgave their iniquity, and did not destroy them. Yes, many a time He turned His anger away, and did not stir up all His wrath.
> —PSALM 78:38

God is compassionate and merciful to all but especially to His covenant people. Israel consistently experienced the compassion of God because of the covenant made with Abraham. God always remembered His covenant and forgave their sins when they repented.

> But you, O Lord, are a God full of compassion, and gracious, longsuffering and abundant in mercy and truth.
> —Psalm 86:15

God's compassion is abundant toward His people. God is plenteous in mercy and truth. God's compassion will come to your family because of Jesus Christ. The more you hear and meditate on these verses, the more faith you will have to experience God's compassion for your loved ones.

> He has made His wonderful works to be remembered; the Lord is gracious and full of compassion.
> —Psalm 111:4

God's compassion is connected to His wonderful works. Israel experienced the wonderful works of God on their behalf through covenant. Believe God for your family members to see and experience the wonderful works of God.

> For He says to Moses, "I will have mercy on whomever I will have mercy, and I will have compassion on whomever I will have compassion."
> —Romans 9:15

God chose Jacob over Esau and had compassion on him. God's compassion on Jacob must be understood in a covenantal context. God's promise to Abraham would be extended to Isaac and Jacob by divine choice (election). Jacob received compassion and was blessed because of this covenant. Esau did not have this covenant and did not receive the blessing of covenant.

Covenant and compassion go hand in hand. Covenant partners will have compassion on one another. Covenant partners will extend mercy to each other. Husbands extend mercy to their wives, wives extend mercy to their husbands, and parents extend mercy to their children.

The compassion of the Lord can be best seen in the story of the prodigal son in Luke chapter 15. The father of the son had compassion on him and received him back home. The story of the prodigal son represents God's love for His children, and God's compassion on them even when they go astray.

God is a father, and He extends mercy to His children. God is concerned about you and your family because God is compassionate toward you. If you are a child of God, you can trust in God's mercy and compassion over your life. God will work on your behalf. God will heal and deliver your loved ones if you ask Him.

Don't underestimate the power of compassion. Compassion is one of the most powerful things in life. Compassion is a force behind miracles. Compassion is the cause of forgiveness. Compassion is the reason the Father sent Jesus. Compassion is a major part of the covenant.

Declare the Lord's Covenant Mercy and Compassion Over Your Family

Lord, I believe You are still moved with compassion today; because of covenant, move on the behalf of my family, in the name of Jesus.

_____

Lord, release Your mercy and compassion upon my loved ones.

_____

Lord, deliver my loved ones from every snare and trap of the enemy through Your compassion.

Lord, heal my loved ones from all sickness and disease through Your compassion.

Lord, I bring my loved ones to You; have compassion on them, and perform miracles in their lives, in the name of Jesus.

Lord, let my loved ones see Your wonderful works in their lives through Your compassion (Ps. 111:4).

Lord, You are plenteous in mercy and truth; let my family members experience Your abundant grace and mercy (Ps. 86:15).

God's mercy is on my family, because we fear Him from generation to generation (Luke 1:50).

God has shown Himself merciful with my family (2 Sam. 22:51).

In the Lord's great mercy He has not consumed or forsaken my family (Neh. 9:31).

My family is ever merciful and lends, and our descendants are blessed (Ps. 37:26).

The Lord has helped my family in remembrance of His mercy (Luke 1:54).

The mercy of the Lord triumphs over judgment for my family (James 2:13).

The Lord shows mercy to my family, because we love Him and keep His commandments (Exod. 20:6).

My family trusts in the mercy of God (Ps. 13:5).

The mercy of the Most High will not be removed from my family (Ps. 21:7).

The Lord remembers His tender mercies and His loving-kindness toward my family, for they are from old (Ps. 25:6).

The Lord will turn Himself to my family and have mercy on us (Ps. 25:16).

The Lord will redeem my family and be merciful to us (Ps. 26:11).

The Lord hears us and will have mercy on our loved ones. He is our helper (Ps. 30:10).

The eye of the Lord is on my family because we fear Him and hope in His mercy (Ps. 33:18).

Blessed is the Lord, who has not turned away the prayers of my loved ones or His mercy from us (Ps. 66:20).

The Lord will show His mercy to my family and will grant us His salvation (Ps. 85:7).

In my family mercy and truth have met together (Ps. 85:10).

The Lord is good to my family. His mercy is everlasting, and His truth endures to all our generations (Ps. 100:5).

The Lord redeems the life of my family from destruction and crowns us with loving-kindness and tender mercies (Ps. 103:4).

For our sake the Lord has remembered His covenant and relented according to the multitude of His mercies (Ps. 106:45).

The Lord is merciful to my family according to His word (Ps. 119:58).

In the Lord's mercy He has cut off the enemies of my family and destroyed all those who afflicted our souls (Ps. 143:12).

Mercy and truth preserve my family (Prov. 20:28).

My family follows righteousness and mercy, and we find life, righteousness, and honor (Prov. 21:21).

Through the Lord's mercies my family is not consumed (Lam. 3:22).

The Dayspring from on high has visited my family, through the tender mercy of our God (Luke 1:78).

The Lord is rich in mercy toward my family because of His great love toward us (Eph. 2:4).

Mercy, peace, and love are multiplied to my family (Jude 2).

The Lord will have mercy on my family, and He will say that we are His people, and we will say He is our God (Hosea 2:23).

In His mercy the Lord led forth my family whom He has redeemed. He has guided us in His strength to His holy habitation (Exod. 15:13).

The Lord is the tower of salvation for my family and shows His mercy to us and our descendants forevermore (2 Sam. 22:51).

My family will give thanks to the Lord, for He is good. His mercy to us endures forever (1 Chron. 16:34).

The Lord will make His face shine on my family and will save us, for His mercies' sake (Ps. 31:16).

The Lord will surround my family with mercy because we trust in Him (Ps. 32:10).

The Lord will let His mercy be upon my family, because we hope in Him (Ps. 33:22).

The God of mercy is a defense for my family. We will sing praise to the Lord, who is our strength (Ps. 59:17).

The faithfulness and mercy of the Lord will be with my family, and in His name our horn shall be exalted (Ps. 89:24).

The Lord will keep His mercy for my family forever, and His covenant will stand firm with us (Ps. 89:28).

The Lord will satisfy my family early with His mercy so that we may rejoice and be glad all our days (Ps. 90:14).

The mercy of the Lord will uphold my loved ones (Ps. 94:18).

The mercy of the Lord is from everlasting to everlasting on my family because we fear Him, and His righteousness to our children's children (Ps. 103:17).

The Lord's merciful kindness will be a comfort for my family (Ps. 119:76).

The Lord's tender mercies are great toward my family, and He will revive us with His judgments (Ps. 119:156).

My family has the mercy of God because we confess and forsake our sins (Prov. 28:13).

Though my family was formerly blasphemers, persecutors, and insolent people, we have obtained the mercy of the Lord, because we did it ignorantly in unbelief (1 Tim. 1:13).

The Lord grants mercy to the households in my family and refreshes them (2 Tim. 1:16).

The Lord will be merciful to the unrighteous in my family. Their sins and lawless deeds He will remember no more (Heb. 8:12).

Just as He forgave the children of Israel, He will pardon the iniquity of my loved ones according to the greatness of His mercy (Num. 14:19).

The Lord our God, the faithful God, keeps His covenant and mercy for a thousand generations of my family because we love Him and keep His commandments (Deut. 4:31).

My family will come into the house of the Lord in the multitude of His mercy, and we will worship toward His holy temple (Ps. 5:7).

Surely goodness and mercy will follow my loved ones all the days of our lives, and we will dwell in the house of the Lord forever (Ps. 23:6).

My family will sing of the mercies of the Lord forever, and with our mouths we will make known His faithfulness to all generations (Ps. 89:1).

The Lord will arise and have mercy on my family, for the time of our favor, yes, the set time, has come (Ps. 102:13).

The eyes of my family look to the Lord our God until He has mercy on us (Ps. 123:2).

The Lord will perfect that which concerns my family. His mercy endures forever. He will not forsake the work of His hands (Ps. 138:8).

The Lord has made an everlasting covenant with my family—the sure mercies of David (Isa. 55:3).

The Lord has betrothed my family. He has betrothed us to Him in righteousness and justice, in loving-kindness and mercy (Hosea 2:19).

My family will sow for themselves in righteousness and reap in mercy (Hosea 10:12).

My family will return to the Lord our God, for He is gracious and merciful, slow to anger, and of great kindness (Joel 2:13).

My loved ones are sick almost unto death, but God will have mercy on them (Phil. 2:27).

The Lord will grant it to my family that we will find mercy from Him in that Day (2 Tim. 1:18).

My family will come boldly to the throne of grace to obtain mercy and help in our time of need (Heb. 4:16).

My family looks for the mercy of the Lord Jesus Christ unto eternal life (Jude 21).

The Lord, in His manifold mercies, did not forsake my family in the wilderness. He has led us and shown us the way we should go (Neh. 9:19).

According to His abundant mercy, the Lord will give my family deliverers who will save us from the hand of our enemies (Neh. 9:27).

My family shall neither hunger nor thirst, neither will heat or sun strike them, for the Lord has mercy on us and will lead us by the springs of water (Isa. 49:10).

The Lord will bring back the captives in my family and have mercy on our whole house, and He will be jealous for us (Ezek. 39:25).

The Lord our God will incline His ear and hear; He will open His eyes and see our desolations, for my family presents our supplications before Him because of His great mercies (Dan. 9:18).

The Lord will strengthen the households in my family. He will bring us back because He has mercy on us. We will not be cast aside. For He is the Lord our God, and He will hear us (Zech. 10:6).

6

PROPHETIC FAMILIES

"As for Me," says the Lord, "this is My covenant with them: My
Spirit who is upon you, and My words which I have put in your
mouth, shall not depart from your mouth, nor from the mouth of
your descendants, nor from the mouth of your descendants' descen-
dants," says the Lord, "from this time and forevermore."

—ISAIAH 59:21

ONE OF THE greatest blessings upon a family through covenant is the gift of the Holy Spirit and the release of the word of the Lord. The word of the Lord brings edification, exhortation, comfort, revelation, impartation, direction, healing, and deliverance. God has promised to put His Spirit upon us and His word in the mouth of our seed and our seed's seed.

We have all seen families that have a godly heritage. Some families have a history of ministers or missionaries who have blessed the world. Some families have tremendous musical gifts that bless the church. Some have released tremendous preachers and teachers. The family unit has been designed by God to be blessed and to be a blessing.

The Holy Spirit can come on your family, and God's word can be in your seed's mouth. The prophetic word releases destiny and purpose. This is often an overlooked part of covenant. Covenant gives us the advantage of hearing and receiving the word of God.

Isaiah spoke of the word of the Lord going from generation to generation. This is a prophetic legacy that can be passed on to the children. Families provide legacy and a framework through which the purposes of God are realized in every generation.

PROPHETIC FAMILIES IN THE BIBLE

> Moreover David and the captains of the army separated for the service some of the sons of Asaph, of Heman, and of Jeduthun, who should prophesy with harps, stringed instruments, and cymbals. And the number of the skilled men performing their service was:
>
> Of the sons of Asaph: Zaccur, Joseph, Nethaniah, and Asharelah; the sons of Asaph were under the direction of Asaph, who prophesied according to the order of the king.
>
> Of Jeduthun, the sons of Jeduthun: Gedaliah, Zeri, Jeshaiah, Shimei, Hashabiah, and Mattithiah, six, under the direction of their father Jeduthun, who prophesied with a harp to give thanks and to praise the Lord.
>
> Of Heman, the sons of Heman: Bukkiah, Mattaniah, Uzziel, Shebuel, Jerimoth, Hananiah, Hanani, Eliathah, Giddalti, Romamti-Ezer, Joshbekashah, Mallothi, Hothir, and Mahazioth.
>
> All these were the sons of Heman the king's seer in the words of God, to exalt his horn. For God gave Heman fourteen sons and three daughters.
>
> —1 CHRONICLES 25:1–5

Not only can the word of the Lord come to your family, but your family can also be prophetic. There are examples of prophetic families in Scripture. There were three prophetic families in the tabernacle of David: the families of Asaph, Jeduthun, and Heman. These families ministered in music and song at the tabernacle. These were musical families that ministered prophetically in worship.

I call these prophetic families ministering before the ark of the

Lord. Heman, the king's seer, had fourteen sons and three daughters. These children were influenced by their father and also carried a prophetic spirit. We can see that there were certain families under the old covenant that had special gifts, including music and prophecy. This is greatly expanded under the new covenant, where everyone has access the Holy Spirit and His gifts to some degree. Now all families of the earth can be blessed.

> And it shall come to pass afterward, that I will pour out my spirit upon *all* flesh; and your sons and your daughters shall prophesy, your old men shall dream dreams, your young men shall see visions.
>
> —Joel 2:28, emphasis added

Joel was prophesying about the new covenant. The new covenant is a covenant of the Holy Spirit. Joel emphasizes the sons and daughters. The Holy Spirit is poured out upon families.

We should expect our sons and daughters to prophesy. Prophecy is a major part of the new covenant. The outpouring of the Holy Spirit at Pentecost was the fulfillment of Joel's prophecy that emphasized the blessing of the sons and daughters.

> The promise is to you and to your children, and to all who are afar off, as many as the Lord our God will call.
>
> —Acts 2:39

God not only saves families, but He also baptizes families with the Holy Spirit. The baptism of the Holy Spirit is the doorway into the prophetic realm.

> Now this man had four virgin daughters who prophesied.
>
> —Acts 21:9

Phillip had four daughters who prophesied. What a powerful prophetic family. This should not be unusual. The Holy Spirit is available to individuals and families.

Children who grow up in an atmosphere of the prophetic can and will receive an impartation. Children carry the prophetic anointing to the next generation. God's covenant is from generation to generation. Children should be encouraged to operate in the prophetic realm. Prophetic parents train and cultivate prophetic children.

> "I raised up some of your sons as prophets, and some of your young men as Nazirites. Is it not so, O you children of Israel?" says the LORD.
>
> —AMOS 2:11

Israel, God's covenant people, saw their sons raised up as prophets. We should also expect God to raise up our children to speak the word of the Lord.

> While Peter was speaking these words, the Holy Spirit fell upon all those who heard the word.
>
> —ACTS 10:44

The household of Cornelius was baptized with the Holy Spirit after hearing Peter preach. This is an example of a Spirit-filled family. Spirit-filled families will be a great witness in the community. These families can release the word of the Lord to their friends and communities. These families will be a great blessing to local churches as well.

PROPHETIC OUTPOUR

An outpour is a large flow or release. Outpour creates an overflow. Overflow speaks of abundance. The outpouring of the Holy Spirit releases an abundance of spiritual grace and gifts in the new covenant. There is an abundance of blessing for any family.

Every family can receive an abundance of grace and gifting because of this outpour. Every member of a family can walk in the prophetic to some degree. Dreams, visions, declaration, prayer, praise, worship, music, dance, counseling, preaching, and teaching can all be aspects of the prophetic realm. God gives liberally and in abundance.

There is no limit to the power that can operate through a family. The new covenant opens the way for all to prosper and prophesy.

TRAIN YOUR CHILDREN IN THE THINGS OF THE SPIRIT

> Train up a child in the way he should go, and when he is old he will not depart from it.
>
> —PROVERBS 22:6

Children should be trained in the things of the Spirit. They should be trained and released in the prophetic. The new covenant releases the Holy Spirit to all believers, and this includes our children. We train our children to minister in the Spirit in our local churches. We don't just entertain our children and keep them busy while their parents attend church. We believe our families should be saved and move in the Spirit.

And the child Samuel ministered unto the LORD before
Eli. And the word of the LORD was precious in those
days; there was no open vision.

—1 SAMUEL 3:1

Samuel began to be trained by the Lord at a young age. He
grew up to be one of Israel's greatest prophets. He then began to
train emerging prophets in Israel. He developed a school for the
prophets and greatly increased the prophetic level in Israel.

Children can be taught to minister to the Lord. Ministering
to the Lord creates an atmosphere for the operation of prophecy.
Churches should be places of ministering to the Lord. Children
and families that live in this kind of atmosphere can expect to
operate in a greater prophetic dimension.

THE PROPHETIC IMPLICATIONS
OF DESTINY AND FATE

God calls individuals and families. Individuals have destiny, and
so do families. I love looking up the etymology of words. Consider
these definitions:

- Destiny: "purpose, intent, fate, destiny; that which
  is destined," noun use of fem. pp. *of destiner*, from
  Latin *destinare* "make firm, establish" (see *destina-
  tion*). The sense is of "that which has been firmly
  established," as by *fate*.[1]

- Fate: "prophetic declaration, oracle, predic-
  tion," thus "that which is ordained, destiny,
  fate," literally "thing spoken (by the gods)," "to
  speak"...The Latin sense evolution is from "sen-
  tence of the Gods" (Greek *theosphaton*) to "lot,

portion" (Greek. *moira*, personified as a goddess in
Homer), also "one of the three goddesses (Clotho,
Lachesis, and Atropos) who determined the course
of a human life."[2]

In any case, notice that *destiny* and *fate* are connected to the
prophetic, even in a pagan sense. Thank God for the *true* prophetic
ministry.

When we think of destiny, we usually think of individuals, but
there is also corporate destiny. Families can also have destiny and
purpose. The prophetic word should be spoken over families as well
as individuals.

I love prophesying over families. I love to minister to the parents and the children. Each individual in the family has a purpose
and a destiny, and the family also has a purpose and a destiny.

And Jacob called his sons and said, "Gather together, that
I may tell you what shall befall you in the last days."
— GENESIS 49:1

Now this is the blessing with which Moses the man of
God blessed the children of Israel before his death.
— DEUTERONOMY 33:1

Another example of individual and corporate destiny can be
seen through the prophecies of Jacob and Moses over the children
of Israel. Israel as a nation had a destiny, but each tribe also had
a destiny.

Each son received a prophetic blessing that shaped destiny.
God's purposes were worked out in these tribes until the coming
of Messiah. This shows the power of the prophetic word upon families and generations. Spirit-filled parents should lay hands on their

children and prophesy. Churches should also provide prophetic ministry for families and teach families how to flow prophetically.

Families should be encouraged to operate in the fullness of the Holy Spirit. It is not enough for one person in the family to be anointed. God will anoint everyone. This is the blessing of covenant. The new covenant opens the way for the Holy Spirit to convict, draw, and anoint individuals and families. Believe God for your family.

> He sent His word and healed them, and delivered them from their destructions.
>
> —Psalm 107:20

> Then the Lord put forth His hand and touched my mouth, and the Lord said unto me: "Behold, I have put My words in your mouth."
>
> —Jeremiah 1:9

Declare the Prophetic Word of the Lord to be Released Over Your Family

Lord, pour out Your Spirit upon my family, and let the sons and daughters prophesy.

Lord, put Your words in the mouth of my seed and my seed's seed.

Let my family members speak Your words with confidence and boldness.

Let the spirit of prophecy be released upon my family members, in the name of Jesus.

Let my family members have dreams and visions by the Spirit of the Lord.

Let the gifts of the Holy Spirit be released in abundance to the members of my family.

Let my family be set in the church and be used by You to minister prophetically.

The word of the Lord has been spoken to all who are in my family (Acts 16:32).

Let the word of the Lord come to my family (Ps. 107:20).

The word of the Lord will be spread out among my family (Acts 13:49).

My family will be numbered according to the word of the Lord (Num. 3:16).

My family will hear the word of the Lord (2 Kings 20:16).

The word of the Lord over my family is right, and all His work is done in truth (Ps. 33:4).

The word of the Lord grows mightily in my family and will prevail (Acts 19:20).

The Lord will reveal Himself to my family by the word of the Lord (1 Sam. 3:21).

The word of the Lord is proven in my family. It is a shield to all of us who trust in Him (2 Sam. 22:31).

My family will go and do according to the word of the Lord (1 Kings 17:5).

My family will inquire for the word of the Lord today (1 Kings 22:5).

The word of the Lord tests my family (Ps. 105:19).

The word of the Lord comes to my family now (Jer. 17:15).

By the word of the Lord that endures forever, the gospel will be preached to my family (1 Pet. 1:25).

All the words that the Lord has said my family will do (Exod. 24:3).

The word of the Lord comes to my family and says, "Do not be afraid. I am your shield, your exceedingly great reward" (Gen. 15:1).

Let the word of the Lord be common among my family. Let there be widespread revelation (1 Sam. 3:1).

The word of the Lord in the mouths of my loved ones is the truth (1 Kings 17:24).

The word of the Lord is with my family (2 Kings 3:12).

The words of the Lord over my family are pure words, like silver tried in a furnace, purified seven times (Ps. 12:6).

Let my family receive the word of the Lord so that we may have wisdom (Jer. 8:9).

The word of the Lord runs swiftly in my family and is glorified (2 Thess. 3:1).

My family shall give heed to the word of the Lord (Jer. 6:10).

The women in my family will hear the word of the Lord and will receive the word of His mouth (Jer. 9:20).

The word of the Lord is with my family, and we make intercession to the Lord of hosts (Jer. 27:18).

My family shall hear the word of the Lord: "You will not die by the sword" (Jer. 34:4).

My family will not suffer a famine of hearing the words of the Lord, in Jesus's name (Amos 8:11).

My family will go to the land of our possession, which we have obtained according to the word of the Lord (Josh. 22:9).

7

THE JOSHUA 1:8 REVELATION

*This Book of the Law shall not depart from your mouth, but
you shall meditate in it day and night, that you may observe to
do according to all that is written in it. For then you will make
your way prosperous, and then you will have good success.*

—JOSHUA 1:8

I N PSALM 25:14 God reveals His promise to show His covenant
to those who fear Him. A revelation of the covenant is one of
the most important revelations one can have. Meditating on
the covenant is an important part of receiving this revelation.

Revelation releases the keys of the kingdom. Jesus gave Peter the
keys of the kingdom after he received a revelation of Christ being
the Son of God. Revelation releases authority and power. The revelation of covenant will cause great power and authority to be released
in your life. Revelation opens up the Word of God and causes you
to see what is hidden from the natural eye. Revelation will give you
understanding of the mysteries of God. You will begin to walk in a
level of understanding that is not common without revelation.

There are many believers who have never heard teaching on covenant and its power in our lives. The covenant is what caused God
to act on behalf of Abraham and his seed. You have a covenant
with God through Jesus Christ that causes God to act on your
behalf. Don't underestimate the power of this covenant.

The more you meditate and hear teaching on covenant, the
more faith you will have in it. I believe this book is helping you
understand covenant and how to apply it to your family. God loves

you, and He loves those who are connected to you. His covenant with you will cause Him to act on the behalf of your loved ones. God is concerned about you and what concerns you. Your concerns will become His concerns because of covenant.

You are not alone in life. You have a covenant partner. You do not have to struggle alone in life. You will see many victories as you understand and walk in faith with your covenant.

God desires for you to understand the covenant. God wants to reveal Himself to you. God will open your eyes to the power of His covenant with you if you ask Him to. Dig into the Word. Dig deep into the covenant. Know your covenant rights and what belongs to you and your family through Jesus Christ. Don't live beneath your privileges. Believe and receive all you have as a result of the covenant you have through Jesus Christ. Meditation will be paramount to this happening with lasting value.

MEDITATION—KEY TO PROSPERITY AND SUCCESS

Joshua 1:8 gives us a key to making one's way prosperous and having good success—*meditating in the Word day and night*. This takes discipline, but it will pay off greatly if done consistently. Prosperity is the key benefit to being in covenant with God.

> In the Old Testament, there are several Hebrew words for the word *meditate*, but the main word is the word *hagah*, which literally means "mutter."
>
> *Hagah* has been translated "mutter" twice (Isa. 59:3; 8:19), "meditate" six times (Josh. 1:8; Ps. 1:2; 63:6; 77:12; 143:5; Isa. 33:18). It has also been translated "speak" four times (Ps. 35:28; 37:30; 115:7; Prov. 8:7), "study" twice (Prov. 15:28; 24:2), "talk" once (Ps. 71:24), and "utter" once (Job 27:4).
>
> It can be noted from these Scriptures that meditation

does indicate the use of the mouth as an instrument to mutter or speak God's Word.[1]

Muttering and meditating upon the Word of God, until it becomes alive in our spirits, is the key to actualizing the promises of God. Muttering (Hebrew *hagah*—mutter) upon the Word of God day and night is likened to a tree planted by the rivers of water absorbing and drawing water into its system through its roots (Ps. 1:3).

> Joshua 1:8 says, "This book of the law shall not depart out of thy mouth." This does not mean you are to keep the Word in your mouth, but rather you are to speak it out your mouth. It should not be away from your lips at any time. Continually speak it. Everyone knows how to mutter. To mutter means to speak things quietly or under your breath, speaking to yourself, regardless of whether people are present to hear you. You may mutter while you are driving your car, or maybe while you are shopping.[2]

The Hebrew word for *mediate* found in Joshua 1:8 is translated "to speak" in the following verses:

- "For my mouth will speak [or meditate] truth" (Prov. 8:7).

- "And my tongue shall speak [or meditate] of Your righteousness and of Your praise all the day long" (Ps. 35:28).

- "The mouth of the righteous speaks [meditates] wisdom, and his tongue talks of judgment" (Ps. 37:30).[3]

Dennis Burke has written a great book called *How to Meditate God's Word*. His teaching likens meditation to chewing the cud:

> To muse means to "ponder, consider, and study closely." This is the aspect of meditation that most people are aware of: taking hold of a promise or a truth and going over it again and again; not going over it in order to memorize it, but squeezing out all the richness; thinking on it and allowing it to wash through your inner man.
>
> The most vivid illustration I can give of musing is a cow chewing her cud. A cow grazes through the pasture, finds an abundance of tasty grass, chews it, and finally swallows it. Later, up comes the chewed grass to chew again (I know what you're thinking...but you have to admit—it is a good example!). Each time the cow brings up the old cud and chews it; she is refining it and making it more and more a part of her system. She chews all the nutrients out of it; the stems and stalk are removed until it is consumed into her body.
>
> This is the most descriptive, powerful example of meditation. Treat the Word of God just as a cow chews her cud. Feed on a scripture over and over again, swallow it, then bring it back up again, going over it again and again. Each time you chew on it, you are demanding all the nutrients out of it, making it more and more a part of your being.[4]

Animals that chew the cud will eat their food, swallow it, and then bring it back up to re-chew it. In this way they get all of the nutrients from what they eat and digest the food into their system in a more complete way. Chewing is of course important to good health and digestion. How many times have our parents told us to chew our food completely?

Meditation is the process of chewing on the Word. We take a

scripture, speak it, think on it, and then we do it again. This is the biblical way to get the Word into our systems and to receive revelation and understanding. *To meditate* means "to ponder, regurgitate, think aloud, consider continuously and utter something over and over again."

This is exactly what we need to do with the Word of God.

> Not without significance, animals in the Old Testament were considered clean and suitable for food if they split the hoof and chewed the cud (Lev. 11:3). By analogy, we could say that a person who "chews the cud" in relation to God's word is made clean and fruitful by the word (John 15:3, 7); just as Christ's glorious church is cleansed by the washing of the water of the word (Eph. 5:26).[5]

> The cow is an animal with four compartments to its stomach, the largest of the four is the rumen, thus these animals are called ruminants. Sheep, goats, bison and deer are other examples of ruminants and this information pertains to them also. The rumen acts somewhat like a large fermentation vat. Inside this vat are bacteria and protozoa that are cellulolytic, meaning they are able to digest cellulose, the major component of plant cell walls. The host animal, in this case the cow, provides the environment for these microbes and they in turn aid in digestion of plant components that the host could not otherwise utilize. These microbes also continue down the digestive tract of the animal where they are digested as part of the protein in the animal's diet. Monogastrics, or single stomached animals like humans and pigs don't have this symbiotic relationship going on to this extent and cannot make good use of the type of plants that cattle typically eat.

> So in cattle, particles of food are bitten off, masticated

to some extent and swallowed. Once a ruminant has eaten, it will go and peacefully stand or lie down while it "chews its cud". I say peacefully because if one is doing it's "cud chewing" it is at ease. The "cud" is actually a portion of regurgitated food that needs shredded into smaller particle for effective digestion in the rumen and beyond.[6]

Rumination—a cow chews something up and stores it up for later. The cow ruminates in perfect timing without waste. She squeezes the nourishment out of it. We transfer the life of Christ into us in a similar manner.

> The dictionary defines "meditate" as to "think about something deeply, to reflect on it or to ponder on it"
> The definition of "muse" however, is not just to meditate on something but to comment upon it, to ruminate upon it—like a cow chewing the cud.[7]

"Meditate" or "muse"—Hebrew word *siyach*—means to put forth, mediate, muse, commune, speak, complain, ponder, sing, to complain, to muse, meditate upon, study, ponder, to talk, sing, speak. Your meditation is also what you are speaking, muttering, singing, complaining about, or pondering.

> Give ear to my words, O LORD, consider my meditation.
> —PSALM 5:1

My meditation is connected to the words of my mouth.

> Let the words of my mouth, and the meditation of my heart be acceptable in Your sight, O LORD, my strength and my Redeemer.
> —PSALM 19:14

> My mouth shall speak of wisdom; and the meditation of my heart shall give understanding.
>
> —Psalm 49:3

My meditation should cause *gladness*.

> May my meditation be sweet to Him; I will be glad in the Lord.
>
> —Psalm 104:34

My meditation is on what I love.

> O how I love Your law! It is my meditation all the day.
>
> —Psalm 119:97

My meditation gives understanding.

> I have more understanding than all my teachers, for Your testimonies are my meditation.
>
> —Psalm 119:99

My meditation brings success.

> This Book of the Law shall not depart from your mouth, but you shall meditate in it day and night, that you may observe to do according to all that is written in it. For then you will make your way prosperous, and then you will have good success.
>
> —Joshua 1:8

My meditation is what I delight in.

> But his delight is in the law of the Lord, and in His law
> he meditates day and night.
>
> —Psalm 1:2

My meditation is at night.

> When I remember You upon my bed, I meditate on You
> in the night watches.
>
> —Psalm 63:6

Meditation Uncovers and Releases God's Wisdom

Joshua 1:8 is the only place the word *success* is found in the King James translation. Success is the Hebrew word *sakal,* meaning to be prudent, be circumspect, to act wisely, to understand, to prosper, give attention to, consider, ponder, to have insight and comprehension.[8]

We can see from this verse that meditation is connected to *wisdom.* Meditation will help you access the wisdom of God. The key to success is wisdom.

Wisdom is one of the greatest benefits of meditating in the Word of God.

> Wisdom is the principal thing; therefore get wisdom. And
> in all your getting, get understanding.
>
> —Proverbs 4:7

Another translation says it this way:

> Getting wisdom is the most important thing you can do.
> Whatever else you get, get insight.
>
> —Proverbs 4:7, gnt

Wisdom is best; wisdom is supreme. Wisdom is the first and primary thing you need to succeed in life.

> Happy is the man that finds wisdom, and the man that gets understanding. For her proceeds are better than the profits of silver, and her gain than fine gold. She is more precious than rubies, and all the things you can desire cannot compare with her. Length of days is in her right hand, in her left hand riches and honor. Her ways are ways of pleasantness, and all her paths are peace. She is a tree of life to those who take hold of her, and happy are all who retain her.
>
> —PROVERBS 3:13–18

These verses emphasize the value of wisdom. It is more precious than rubies. Nothing compares to wisdom. Wisdom results in long life. Wisdom brings you to riches and honor. Wisdom leads to peace. Wisdom promotes happiness. This is what biblical meditation will produce in your life. Wisdom produces riches and honor. Wisdom will cause you to inherit substance. Wisdom will fill your treasures. (See Proverbs 8:18–21.)

When you find wisdom, you will find life. You will obtain the favor of the Lord (Prov. 8:35). This is also in line with the benefits of being in covenant with God.

TEACH YOUR CHILDREN TO MEDITATE ON THE COVENANT PROMISES OF GOD

Covenant promises require obedience and holiness. Children need to be taught to walk in the ways of the Lord. Secure the covenant in your family for generations to come by teaching your children to meditate on the Word of God.

For I have known him, in order that he may command his children and his household after him, that they keep the way of the LORD, to do righteousness and justice, that the LORD may bring to Abraham what He has spoken to him.
—GENESIS 18:19

You shall teach them to your children, speaking of them when you sit in your house, when you walk by the way, when you lie down, and when you rise up. And you shall write them on the doorposts of your house and on your gates, that your days and the days of your children may be multiplied in the land of which the LORD swore to your fathers to give them, like the days of the heavens above the earth.
—DEUTERONOMY 11:19–21
(SEE ALSO DEUTERONOMY 6:7–9)

Train up a child in the way he should go, and when he is old he will not depart from it.
—PROVERBS 22:6

And you, fathers, do not provoke your children to wrath, but bring them up in the training and admonition of the Lord.
—EPHESIANS 6:4

DECLARE THE BENEFITS OF MEDITATION FOR COVENANT REVELATION OVER YOUR FAMILY

My family will meditate also on all the Lord's work and talk of His doings (Ps. 77:12).

My family will meditate on the Lord's precepts and contemplate His ways (Ps. 119:15).

Princes also did sit and speak against my family, but we did meditate on the Lord's statutes (Ps. 119:23).

Let the proud be ashamed; for they dealt perversely with me without a cause, but I will meditate on Your precepts (Ps. 119:78).

The eyes of my family are awake during the night watches so that we may meditate on the Lord's word (Ps. 119:148).

My family will meditate upon these things and give ourselves entirely to them so that our progress may be evident to all (1 Tim. 4:15).

My family loves the law of the Lord; it is our mediation all the day (Ps. 119:97).

The law of the Lord is my family's delight, and in His law we meditate day and night (Ps. 1:2).

My family shall be made to understand the way of the Lord's precepts, so we shall meditate on His wonderful works (Ps. 119:27).

My family will remember the days of old and meditate on all the Lord's works. We will muse on the work of Your hands (Ps. 143:5)

My family will lift our hands up to the Lord's commandments, which we love, and we will meditate on His statutes (Ps. 119:48).

A book of remembrance will be written for my family, who fears the Lord and meditates on His name (Mal. 3:16).

My family will mediate on the Book of the Law day and night (Josh. 1:8).

8

CONTEND FOR THE COVENANT
THROUGH FASTING AND PRAYER

*Now in the twenty-fourth day of this month the children of Israel
were assembled with fasting, in sackcloth, and with dust upon
their head. . . . "And because of all this, we make a sure covenant
and write it; our leaders, our Levites, and our priests, seal it."*

—NEHEMIAH 9:1, 38

ASTING IS A way we can renew covenant with the Lord. Fasting helps fallen believers become restored. Fasting is a part of renewing our commitment to the things of God. Fasting has great rewards. Many believers are unaware of the great rewards that come through fasting. Understanding the great benefits of fasting will motivate more believers to make it a regular part of their lives.

Fasting is also one of the ways to increase the breaker anointing. Do you have things in your life or in the lives of your family members that need to be broken? Fasting can release the breaker anointing. The prophet Micah prophesied the day of the breaker coming up before his people. We are living in the days of the breaker.

> The one who breaks open will come up before them; they will break out, pass through the gate, and go out by it; their king will pass before them, with the LORD at their head.
>
> —MICAH 2:13

The Lord is a breaker. He is able to break through any obstacle or opposition on behalf of His covenant people. There is a breaker anointing arising upon the church. We are seeing and experiencing more breakthroughs than ever before. Fasting will cause breakthroughs to continue in families, cities, nations, finances, church growth, salvation, healing, and deliverance. It will help believers to break through all opposition from the enemy.

There are some spirits operating in our families that cannot be overcome without fasting. Some believers struggle with certain limitations that they cannot seem to break through. A revelation for how covenant and fasting work hand in hand will change this and result in victories that would not ordinarily be obtained. A life of consistent fasting will cause many victories to manifest. God's will is that His covenant believers live a life of victory and perfect peace with nothing being impossible to them.

As we learn from Matthew 17:21, there are stubborn spirits that will only respond to fasting and prayer. These tend to be the generational strongholds that tenaciously hold on to families and nations for years. Fasting will break these strongholds. These strongholds include poverty, sickness, witchcraft, sexual impurity, pride, fear, confusion, and marital problems. Fasting will help a believer to overcome these strongholds and break free from their limitations.

Approach Fasting With Humility and Sincerity

In Jesus's day the Pharisees fasted with attitudes of pride and superiority:

> The Pharisee stood and prayed thus with himself, "God, I thank You that I am not like other men...I fast twice a week..."
>
> —LUKE 18:11–12

This approach is not acceptable to God. Fasting must be genuine and not religious or hypocritical. God requires humility and sincerity in fasting. We must have correct motives in fasting. Fasting is a powerful tool if done correctly. Muslims and Hindus fast, but their fasts are merely religious.

Isaiah chapter 58 describes the fast that God has chosen:

- Fasting cannot be done with amusement (v. 3).
- Fasting cannot be done while mistreating others (v. 3).
- Fasting cannot be done for strife or contention (v. 4).
- Fasting should cause one to bow his head in humility, like a bulrush (v. 5).
- Fasting should be a time of searching the heart and repenting.
- Fasting should be done in an attitude of compassion for the lost and hurting (v. 7).

This is the fast that God promises to bless.

The enemy knows the power of prayer and fasting, and he will do everything in his power to stop you. Believers who begin to fast can expect to encounter much spiritual resistance. A believer must be committed to a fasted lifestyle. The rewards of fasting far outweigh the obstacles of the enemy.

HOW TO FAST

Fasting is beneficial whether you fast partially or fully. One-day fasts on a consistent basis will strengthen your spirit over time and give you the ability to discipline yourself for longer fasts. Three-day fasts with just water are a powerful way to see breakthroughs. Fasts longer than three days should be done by people with more experience in fasting.

I do not recommend long fasts unless there is an emergency or if one is led by the Holy Spirit to do so. Daniel fasted twenty-one days and saw a great breakthrough for his people (Dan. 9–10). Daniel was also a prophet, and God will use prophets to fast for different reasons to see breakthroughs. Jesus fasted forty days before beginning His ministry. I do know of people who have fasted forty days and have seen great breakthroughs.

A partial fast can include some food such as vegetables and can be done for long lengths. Complete fasts consist of water only, and water is important to cleanse the system of toxins that are released through fasting. The Holy Spirit will reveal to you when you need to fast. A fasted lifestyle is a powerful lifestyle.

THE BENEFITS OF FASTING FOR BREAKTHROUGH IN YOUR FAMILY

As we have already discussed, because you walk in covenant with God, you have a promise that your whole household will be saved. But if you also want to see your family manifest the full benefits and blessing of covenant, you can also begin to fast and pray for breakthrough in the many areas that your family struggles with. Fasting will break poverty, sickness, division and strife, sexual impurity, pride, fear, confusion, vicious cycles, and more off of your family. Here is what you can expect to see as a covenant believer fasting for your family.

Fasting will break the spirit of poverty in your family, and it prepares the way for prosperity (Joel 2:15, 18–19, 24–26).

The prophet Joel gave the people the proper response to the locust invasion. Locusts represent demons that devour. Locusts represent the spirits of poverty and lack. The locusts had come upon Israel and devoured the harvest. Joel encouraged the people to fast and repent. God promised to hear their prayer and answer by sending corn, wine, and oil.

Corn, wine, and oil represent prosperity, one of the signs of walking in covenant with God. Fasting breaks the spirit of poverty and releases the spirit of prosperity. I have seen countless numbers of believers struggle in the area of their finances. Prosperity is elusive to many. This is because the demons of poverty have not been bound through fasting and prayer.

In Deuteronomy 8:3, 7–9, 18 God allowed the people to hunger in the wilderness by feeding them with only manna. They ate manna for forty years. This preceded their entering the Promised Land. Fasting helps prepare a believer for the good land. This is a land without scarceness. This is a land with no lack. Fasting humbles the soul (Ps. 35:13). God rewards those who fast (Matt. 6:18). Tremendous blessings are released for those who understand the power of fasting and do it.

Fasting is one of the ways we can break generational strongholds of poverty. Fasting prepares a believer for prosperity by bringing them into a place of humility. God has promised to exalt the humble (1 Pet. 5:6). Financial promotion is part of this exaltation. God gives grace (favor) to the humble (James 4:6). Favor is a part of financial prosperity. Fasting releases grace and favor upon a person's life. This will break the cycle of poverty and failure.

Fasting will break the power of fear that oppresses members of your family (Joel 2:21).

Do you desire to see great things happen in your life and in your family? The Lord desires to do great things for His covenant people. Fasting will break the spirit of fear in your life and in your family's life and will prepare the way for great things to happen. These great things include signs and wonders.

Fasting will release the Holy Spirit and increase prophetic anointing in your family (Joel 2:28).

In chapter 6 I talked about the power of prophetic families. Fasting will help to release power of the prophetic anointing over your family through the Holy Spirit. This is one of the greatest promises given by the prophet Joel, that God would pour out His spirit over your family, and they will prophesy, dream dreams, and see visions. This is the promise of the last-day outpouring of the Holy Spirit. Fasting helps to release the manifestation of prophecy. Fasting also helps release visions and dreams. The word of the Lord is health and life to a family unit.

Fasting will break the stronghold of sexual impurity operating in your family.

Sexual sin is one of the hardest sins to break. Many believers struggle with generational lusts that have passed down through the family lines. Lust spirits cause much shame, guilt, and condemnation. This robs the believers of the confidence and boldness he should have as a believer. Many believers struggle with masturbation, pornography, perversion, and fornication. Fasting for your family will drive these generational spirits from their life.

In Judges 19:22 we read about some men in a city who wanted to have sexual relations with the guest of an old man in that city. They were homosexuals who were identified as sons of Belial. The man of the house tried to discourage them and offered them his daughter and the guest's concubine instead. The men took the concubine of the guest and abused her all night. The abuse was so severe that she died. The guest then took a knife and cut the concubine into twelve pieces and sent them to every tribe in Israel. His concubine had been raped to death.

The men who raped the concubine were from the tribe of Benjamin. The men of Israel gathered against the city and requested they turn over the guilty men. The children of Benjamin would not listen and instead gathered themselves to battle. The children of Benjamin then destroyed twenty-two thousand men of Israel on the first day (Judges 20:21), and they destroyed eighteen thousand on the second day (v. 25).

> Then all the children of Israel, that is, all the people, went up and came unto the house of God and wept. They sat there before the LORD and fasted that day until evening; and they offered burnt offerings and peace offerings before the LORD.... The LORD defeated Benjamin before Israel.
>
> —JUDGES 20:26, 35

Israel could not overcome Benjamin until they fasted. The resistance of Benjamin implies that there was something demonic behind them. Twelve tribes could not overcome one tribe because of this demonic resistance. This resistance was broken after fasting. This was the only way perversion was rooted out of the tribe of Benjamin. Fasting helps you and your family break free from the chains of sexual perversion and lust.

Fasting will break the power of sickness and infirmity and release healing in your family (Isa. 58:5–6, 8).

Many families suffer from hereditary illnesses or germs and bacteria that pass from one family member to the next. People are always hearing about one family member or another being ill. Diseases such as cancer, diabetes, high blood pressure, sinus problems, and chronic pain are spirits of infirmity that are often generational. Fasting helps eliminate chronic sickness and diseases. God has promised that our health will spring forth speedily.

Fasting will release God's glory for your protection (Isa. 58:8).

Divine protection is another promise from Isaiah 58. God promises to protect us with His glory. Fasting releases the glory of the Lord, which covers us and our families. God has promised to cover the church with glory as a defense (Isa. 4:5). The enemy cannot penetrate or overcome this glory.

Fasting will result in answered prayer for your family (Isa. 58:9).

Demonic interference causes many prayers to be hindered. Daniel fasted twenty-one days to break through demonic resistance and receive answers to his prayers. (See Daniel 10.) The prince of Persia withstood the answers for twenty-one days. Daniel's fast helped an angel to break through and bring the answers.

Fasting will cause many answers to prayer to be accelerated. These include prayers for salvation of loved ones and deliverance. Fasting helps to break the frustration of unanswered prayer.

Fasting releases divine guidance for matters that concern you and your family (Isa. 58:11).

Many believers have difficulty making correct decisions concerning relationships, finances, and ministry. This causes setbacks and wasted time because of foolish decisions. Fasting will help believers make correct decisions by releasing divine guidance. Fasting eliminates confusion. Fasting causes clarity and releases understanding and wisdom to make correct decisions.

Fasting is recommended for those who are making important decisions such as marriage and ministry choices.

Fasting will break generational curses in your family (Isa. 58:12).

Many of the obstacles believers encounter are generational. Generational curses result from the iniquity of the fathers. Generational sins such as pride, rebellion, idolatry, witchcraft, occult involvement, Masonry, and lust open the door for evil spirits to operate in families through generations. Demons of destruction, failure, poverty, infirmity, lust, and addiction are major strongholds in the lives of millions of people.

Fasting helps loose the bands of wickedness. Fasting lets the oppressed go free. Fasting helps us to rebuild the old waste places. Fasting reverses the desolation that results from sin and rebellion.

Fasting closes breaches and brings forth restoration and rebuilding to your family (Isa. 58:12; Neh. 1:4).

There are many believers who need restoration. They need restoration in their families, finances, relationships, health, and walk with the Lord. Fasting is a part of restoration.

Fasting closes the breaches. Breaches are gaps in the wall that give the enemy an entry point into our lives. Breaches need to be repaired and closed. When the breaches are closed, the enemy no longer has as opening to attack.

Fasting also helps keep us on the right path (Isa. 58:12). Fasting helps to prevent us from going astray. Fasting will help those who have strayed from the right path to return. Fasting is a cure for backsliding.

Fasting helps us to walk in the good path (Prov. 2:9), the path of life (Prov. 2:19), the path of peace (Prov. 3:17), the old path (Jer. 6:16), and the straight path (Heb. 12:13). Fasting restores these paths and helps us to walk in them.

In Nehemiah 1 we see that Nehemiah's journey to restore and rebuild the walls in Jerusalem began with fasting. Fasting initiated the events that made his plans possible. Fasting will be an asset to anyone with a desire to see restoration in the lives of people who have experienced desolation.

Fasting helps restore and rebuild the walls in our lives that have been broken down. Walls are symbolic of protection and safety. A city without walls is open for attack from the enemy (Prov. 25:28). Fasting helps restore the walls of salvation (Isa. 60:18). Fasting helps restore watchmen to the walls (Isa. 62:6).

Fasting will cause you and your family to have great victory against overwhelming odds (2 Chron. 20:3).

Jehoshaphat was facing the combined armies of Moab, Ammon, and Edom. He was facing overwhelming odds. Fasting helped him to defeat these enemies. Fasting helps us to have victory in the midst of defeat.

Jehoshaphat called a fast because he was afraid. Fear is another stronghold that many believers have difficulty overcoming. Fasting will break the power of the demon of fear. Spirits of terror, panic, fright, apprehension, and timidity can be overcome through fasting. Freedom from fear is a requirement to live a victorious lifestyle.

Fasting will prepare the way for you and your children and delivers you from enemies that lie in wait (Ezra 8:21, 31).

The prophet Ezra fasted because he recognized the danger of his mission. Fasting will protect you and your children from the plans of the enemy. Fasting will stop the ambush of the enemy. Fasting will cause your substance to be protected from the attack of the enemy.

Fasting will break the powers of carnality, division, and strife in your family (Phil. 3:19).

Carnality is a problem in many families in the body of Christ. To be carnal means to be fleshly. It means to mind earthly things. We should not be controlled by the belly. Fasting takes the power away from the belly and strengthens the spirit.

To be carnally minded is death. To be spiritually minded is life and peace (Rom. 8:6). Carnality causes division and strife (1 Cor. 3:3). Carnality hinders believers from growing and coming into maturity. Carnality prevents believers from understanding the deeper truths of the Scriptures.

Fasting helps believers focus on spiritual things. Fasting breaks us free from the power of the flesh. Fasting increases spiritual discernment (1 Cor. 2:15).

Fasting will break the powers of pride, rebellion, and witchcraft in your family (Ps. 35:13; Job 33:17–20).

Sickness can be a result of pride. Pain can also be a result of pride. Sickness often results in the loss of appetite. This is a forced fast. Fasting humbles the soul. Fasting helps us overcome the strongman of pride. Pride and rebellion are generational spirits that are often difficult to overcome.

Gluttony and drunkenness are signs of rebellion (Deut. 21:20). Rebellion is as the sin of witchcraft (1 Sam. 15:23). God humbled Israel in the wilderness by feeding them with only manna (Deut. 8:3). Israel lusted for meat in the wilderness. This was a manifestation of rebellion (Ps. 106:14–15).

Fasting will cause the joy and the presence of the Lord to return to your family (Mark 2:20).

The presence of the bridegroom causes joy. Weddings are filled with joy and celebration. When a believer loses joy and the presence of the Lord, he or she needs to fast. Fasting causes the joy and presence of the Lord to return. No believer can live a victorious life without the presence of the bridegroom. The joy of the Lord is our strength (Neh. 8:10).

Fasting will release the power of the Holy Spirit for the miraculous to occur in your family (Luke 4:14, 18).

Fasting increases the anointing and the power of the Holy Spirit in the life of a believer. Jesus ministered in power after fasting. He healed the sick and casted out devils. All believers are expected to do the same works (John 14:12). Fasting helps us to minister healing and deliverance to our families and others around us. Fasting helps us walk in the power of God. Fasting releases the anointing for miracles to happen in your life and your family's lives.

DECLARE THE BENEFITS OF FASTING OVER YOUR FAMILY

Lord, I believe in the power of Your chosen fast (Isa. 58).

Lord, let my fasting destroy the yokes that the enemy has set up in my family.

Let Your light come into my family through Your chosen fast.

Let health and healing be released to my family though Your chosen fast.

Be my family's reward through Your chosen fast.

Let me see breakthroughs of salvation and deliverance in my family through Your chosen fast.

Let miracles be released on the behalf of my loved ones through Your chosen fast.

Let Your power and authority be released on the behalf of my family through Your chosen fast.

I humble my soul through fasting; let Your favor exalt me.

I drive every stubborn demon out of my family through Your chosen fast.

Let Your covenant blessing and mercy be released on my loved ones through Your chosen fast.

Nothing is impossible with You, Lord; let my impossibilities become possibilities through Your chosen fast.

Let every assignment of hell against my family be broken through Your chosen fast.

Let all pride, rebellion, and witchcraft operating in my family be destroyed through Your chosen fast.

Let Your anointing increase in my life through Your chosen fast.

Let my family enjoy restoration through Your chosen fast.

Let all carnality be rebuked from my family through Your chosen fast.

Let all habits and iniquity in my family be broken and overcome through Your chosen fast.

Let my prayers for my loved ones be answered speedily through Your chosen fast.

Guide me and my family members through Your chosen fast.

Manifest Your glory to my family through Your chosen fast.

Let the strongholds of sexual impurity and lust be broken in my family through Your chosen fast.

Let sickness and infirmity be destroyed in my family, and let healing come forth through Your chosen fast.

Let all poverty and lack be destroyed in my family through Your chosen fast.

Remove all oppression and torment from the enemy in my family through Your chosen fast.

My family fasted and petitioned the Lord, and He answered our prayer (Ezra 8:23).

After we fast and pray, we will lay hands on those in our family and send them (Acts 13:3).

My family will fast without quarreling and strife, and in striking each other with wicked fists, so in the end our voice will be heard on high (Isa. 58:4).

When we fast we will anoint our heads and wash our faces. We will not be hypocrites with sad countenances (Matt. 6:16–17).

My family humbles themselves with fasting (Ps. 35:13).

My family will turn to the Lord with fasting, weeping, and mourning (Joel 2:12).

My family will consecrate a fast and call a sacred assembly (Joel 2:15).

This "kind" that my family faces will go out from among us through our fasting and prayer (Matt. 17:21).

Through prayer and fasting we have appointed leaders among our family and have commended them to the Lord (Acts 14:23).

My family will not exploit our laborers, so that in the day we fast, the Lord will see and take notice (Isa. 58:3).

My family will fast according the fast chosen by the Lord (Isa. 58:5).

My family will fast for the Lord (Zech. 7:5).

I will gather my family, and we will fast so that we may approach the King (Esther 4:16).

My family will fast and lay on the ground all night, pleading with God for our children (2 Sam. 12:16).

My family will fast and weep for our children (2 Sam. 12:21).

My family will proclaim a fast and humble ourselves before our God, to seek from Him the right way for us and our little ones and all our possessions (Ezra 8:21).

My family will arise from fasting, fall on our knees, and spread out our hands to the Lord our God (Ezra 9:5).

My family will fast and pray before the God of heaven (Neh. 1:4).

My family will assemble with fasting, in sackcloth, and dust on our heads (Neh. 9:1).

My family fasts to loose the bonds of wickedness, to undo heavy burdens, to the let the oppressed go free, and to break every yoke (Isa. 58:6).

My family will spend the night in fasting (Dan. 6:18).

My family will set our faces toward the Lord God to make requests by prayer and supplication, with fasting, sackcloth, and ashes (Dan. 9:3).

My family believes God, and we will proclaim a fast from the least to the greatest of us, and the Lord will hear our cries of repentance and relent of the disaster meant for us (Jon. 3:5, 10).

My family fasts in the secret place, and our Father sees in secret. He will reward us openly (Matt. 6:18).

My family will not depart from the temple of the Lord, but we will serve God with fasting and prayers night and day (Luke 2:37).

NOTES

CHAPTER ONE
GOD BLESSES FAMILIES THROUGH HIS COVENANT

1. J. E. Leonard, *I Will Be Their God* (Hamilton, IL: Laudement Press, 2012).
2. Preceptaustin.org, "Covenant Definition," http://preceptaustin.org/covenant_definition.htm (accessed February 27, 2013).
3. James W. Goll, *Deliverance From Darkness* (Grand Rapids, MI: Chosen, 2010), 168–169.
4. Ibid., 168.
5. Encountersnetwork.com, "Generational Blessings," http://www.encountersnetwork.com/email_blasts/June_2005_EN_GB.html (accessed February 27, 2013).
6. Ibid.

CHAPTER TWO
GOD VISITS FAMILIES

1. Blue Letter Bible, "Dictionary and Word Search for *episkeptomai* (Strong's 1980)" http://www.blueletterbible.org/lang/lexicon/lexicon.cfm?Strongs=G1980&t=KJV (accessed February 27, 2013).
2. Dictionary.com, s.v. "visit," http://dictionary.reference.com/browse/visits (accessed February 27, 2013).
3. J. I. Packer, *Your Father Loves You* (n.p.: Harold Shaw Publishers, 1986).

CHAPTER THREE
A LAMB FOR A HOUSE

1. Traditional-American-Values.com, "About Family: the Family in America Today," http://traditional-american-values.com/family-values/ (accessed February 28, 2013).

CHAPTER FOUR
DELIVERANCE AND HEALING FOR FAMILIES

1. "God, Save My Family," Sonlight Ministries Devotional, http://sonlightdevotional.org/library/stories/redemptive-power/god-save-my-family/ (accessed January 15, 2013). Permission requested.
2. Portions of this chapter were adapted from John Eckhardt, *Prayers That Bring Healing* (Lake Mary, FL: Charisma House, 2010).

CHAPTER FIVE
THE COVENANTAL MERCY OF GOD

1. Blue Letter Bible, "Dictionary and Word Search for *checed* (Strong's 2617)," http://www.blueletterbible.org/lang/lexicon/lexicon.cfm?strongs=H2617 (accessed March 1, 2013).
2. Blue Letter Bible, "Dictionary and Word Search for *racham* (Strong's 7355)," http://www.blueletterbible.org/lang/lexicon/lexicon.cfm?strongs=H7355 (accessed March 1, 2013).

CHAPTER SIX
PROPHETIC FAMILIES

1. Online Etymology Dictionary, s.v. "destiny," http://www.etymonline.com/index.php?allowed_in_frame=0&search=destiny&searchmode=none (accessed March 1, 2013).
2. Online Etymology Dictionary, s.v. "fate," http://www.etymonline.com/index.php?term=fate (accessed March 1, 2013).

CHAPTER SEVEN
THE JOSHUA 1:8 REVELATION

1. Peter Tan, *Meditation on God's Word* (Belconnen, Australia: Peter Tan Evangelism, 2008), 4, http://spiritword.net/ebooks/Foundational_Truth01.pdf (accessed March 1, 2013).
2. Dennis Burke, *How to Meditate God's Word* (Arlington, TX: Dennis Burke Publications, 1982).
3. Ibid.

4. Ibid. Permission requested.

5. Olive Tree Learning Center, "Meditating on God's Word," http://www.olivetree.com/learn/articles/meditating-on-gods-word.php (accessed March 4, 2013).

6. Greenvistafarm.com, "Animal Benefits: Animal Benefits of a 100% Forage Diet," http://www.greenvistafarm.com/animal.html (accessed March 4, 2013).

7. Tom Smith, "Discovering the Lost Art of Musing on the Word of God," Holdingtotruth.com, http://holdingtotruth.com/2012/05/07/discovering-the-lost-art-of-musing-on-the-word-of-god/ (accessed March 4, 2013).

8. Blue Letter Bible, "Dictionary and Word Search for *sakal* (Strong's 7919)," http://www.blueletterbible.org/lang/lexicon/lexicon.cfm?Strongs=H7919&t=KJV (accessed March 4, 2013).